PRESERVING FRUITS & VEGETABLES

THE WELL-STOCKED PANTRY

PRESERVING FRUITS & VEGETABLES

Carol W. Costenbader

A Storey Publishing Book

STOREY

Storey Communications, Inc.
Schoolhouse Road
Pownal, Vermont 05261

*The mission of Storey Communications is to serve our customers
by publishing practical information that encourages personal
independence in harmony with the environment.*

United States edition published in 1996 by
Storey Communications, Inc.
Schoolhouse Road, Pownal, Vermont 05261

Produced by Weldon Russell Pty Ltd
43 Victoria Street
McMahons Point, NSW 2060, Australia

A member of the Weldon Owen Group of Companies

© Weldon Russell Pty Ltd 1996

Chief Executive: Elaine Russell
Publisher: Karen Hammial
Managing Editor: Ariana Klepac
Project Co-ordinator: Megan Johnston
Editors: Libby Frederico, Kayte Nunn
Editorial Assistants: Elizabeth Connolly, Cassandra Sheridan
Designer: Honor Morton
Illustrator: James Gordon
Food Stylists: Penny Farrell, Kay Francis
Photographers: John Callanan, John Hollingshead
Production: Dianne Leddy

Special thanks to Lynda Spivey, CHE, Home Economics Extension
Agent, North Carolina Cooperative Extension Service.

Produced by Mandarin Offset, Hong Kong
Printed in China

Library of Congress Cataloging-in-Publication Data
Costenbader, Carol W.
    Preserving fruits & vegetables / Carol W. Costenbader.
       p.   cm. — (The well-stocked pantry)
    Includes bibliographical references and index.
    ISBN 0-88266-852-8 (hardcover)
    1. Fruit—Preservation 2. Vegetables—Preservation
      I. Title. II. Series.
    TX612.F7C657 1996
    641.4—dc20   95–42379
                 CIP

Contents

INTRODUCING THE BASICS 8

FREEZING FRUITS AND VEGETABLES
Introduction 14
Recipes 20
Freezing Chart 34

DRYING FRUITS AND VEGETABLES
Introduction 38
Recipes 43
Drying Chart 52

CANNING FRUITS AND VEGETABLES
Introduction 56
Recipes 62
Hot-water Canning Chart 92
Pressure Canning Chart 93

Mail Order Sources 94
Index 95

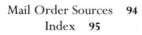

Introducing the Basics

$\mathscr{T}$his book provides a creative answer to preserving fruits and vegetables in times of abundance, making them available on your pantry shelf in times of need. The new, exciting, fully-tested recipes are all described in easy-to-follow steps, and comply with the United States Department of Agriculture (USDA) and the corresponding Canadian government guidelines.

From freezing to drying to canning (bottling), together with seasonal tips and gift-giving ideas, *Preserving Fruits & Vegetables* is the perfect guide for the adventurous cook. The charts at the end of each chapter offer quick references but are not meant to take the place of text. Read carefully all information on your particular subject matter before beginning any preserving project. Start reading in winter, training your eye to look for nature's seasonal bounty as it begins appearing in spring!

Choosing and Handling the Harvest

Extending the life of produce so that a plentiful supply is available all year round . . . that's what the well-stocked pantry is all about. When the harvest begins to ripen in full force, there's no need to spend all day "putting up" vegetables and fruits for the pantry or freezer. Instead, I pick what is ready from my garden, usually enough for two or three meals. I prefer to preserve fruits and vegetables prepared to a state ready to defrost, heat, and serve, or, in the case of canned (bottled) goods, just heat and serve. My dinner is

automatically planned for the day and is dictated by what produce I find in the garden on an early morning visit. I usually make three casseroles — one for dinner and two for the freezer. Those not fortunate enough to live with a keen gardener can take advantage of the abundance available at farmer's markets or even the grocery store. In spring I look for Vidalia (sweet salad) onions, available for only a short while and not suited to long cold storage. The sweet pungent flavor freezes beautifully when cooked in casserole form. In summer I can count on an herbed zucchini (courgette) casserole for the freezer as well as peach and blackberry crumb "pie" with no bottom crust. I freeze in glass pie plates lined with heavy duty aluminum foil. When the food is frozen hard, remove the glass plate to save space and stack in the freezer in labeled, dated freezer bags; when wanted, remove the foil and slip the food back onto the plate to thaw and cook. When Roma tomatoes are in season, it's time to dry a few for Christmas gifts. Sometimes I have five or six projects going at once. It takes only a little time each day once you get started.

Toward the end of summer when nature is bursting in abundance, I get out my pressure canner (bottler) and make a vegetable soup base, using everything available, to be eventually enjoyed on a cold day in winter. Usually vegetables need to be harvested when fairly young. Select your corn and peas while still sweet and newly picked, green beans when tender and small, and squash while the skins are relatively thin. However, most fruit is best when completely ripe and the sugar content is highest, especially for canning and freezing.

All fresh produce preserves best when it is prepared immediately or as soon as possible after harvest. The time between harvest and preservation is very important as many chemical changes can take place in the fruits or vegetables. Insure that you wash all produce well and carefully, being certain not to bruise and break. Keep all work surfaces, dish towels, equipment, and your hands perfectly clean and hygienic.

Do not leave the fresh produce at room temperature if you can't preserve it right away. Instead, refrigerate it, even if only for a few hours. If you have gone to the effort to buy or grow the best, don't ruin it by not preparing it for preserving immediately. If you buy at the farmer's market, don't leave it in a hot car and run other errands.

ABOUT INGREDIENTS

SALT Salt is for flavoring only in canned foods, it is not a preservative agent. Canning or pickling salt is pure. Table salt may contain iodine and other agents to prevent caking. Canning salt also contains anti-caking agents and has the same density for measuring as table salt.

Brine solution is simply salt dissolved in liquid. The brine solution is achieved by adding canning salt by weight to the proper volume of liquid. The percentage of brine can allow proper fermentation or, if high enough (greater than 15 percent), can actually control the growth of salt-tolerant bacteria.

Do not use salt substitutes in canning. Add substitutes for flavor when serving only.

RECOMMENDED SUGAR AND SWEETENERS Following are the various kinds of sweetening agents that may be used:

Table Sugar — Generally use granulated table (beet or cane) sugar, unless otherwise instructed. The sugar in jams and jellies helps the pectin in the mixture to set up or gel and enhances the flavor. In larger quantities (more than 65 percent), sugar actually acts as a preservative. One teaspoon has 18 calories (75 kilojoules). Table sugar is also called sucrose.

Light Corn Syrup — Light corn syrup enhances the gloss of jams and jellies. Substitute 25 percent of the sugar called for in a recipe with light corn syrup. One teaspoon has 20 calories (84 kilojoules). Light corn syrup is also called glucose.

Honey — Light, mild honey can be used up to 50 percent as a replacement for sugar quantities. It has double the sweetening power of white table sugar. Recipes will have to be cooked for about 8–10 minutes longer, but not more than 20 minutes, depending

on whether the recipe uses pectin or is a cook-down variety. Recipes will be a bit thicker. Honey is approximately 60 percent fructose and 40 percent glucose.

Aspartame — This artificial non-nutritive sweetener can be used in some recipes to equal the amount of sugar called for. Be certain to add at the last stage after mixing. This product can only be used in uncooked freezer fruit recipes. It is not recommended for canned fruit because it breaks down upon prolonged heating.

WATER Water must be drinkable and have no off odors or flavors.

SPICES Never use last year's half-filled spice can for this season's tastiest result. Whole pungent new spices, tied in a cheesecloth (muslin) bag, are best for preserving. Ground spices can cloud and detract from the finished product. Remove the spice bag after filling the jars.

OILS Tasting oils is like sampling wines. From the fruity green of olive oil to the pale neutral of safflower oil to the richness of pungent oils from hazelnuts, walnuts and so on, the possibilities are endless. Oils are used to carry the flavors of salad dressings, pickles, or whatever the recipe specifies. Always store oils in a cool place. Try to buy cold-pressed oils as usually they have a better flavor. After 6 months oils can become rancid. Always check first before using in recipes. You'll want to try many different ones until you discover the range of flavors that suits you best.

VINEGARS Vinegars are produced by allowing an alcoholic liquid to be oxidized by a process in which the alcohol is transformed into acetic acid. They vary slightly in taste and acidity. Avoid metal containers (other than stainless steel) when using vinegar for preserving. Make certain you have a stainless steel or enameled canner or ceramic crock. Use white vinegars when the brown or red kind would spoil the color of the finished product. White distilled vinegar is relatively low in acid (4–6 percent acetic acid). Cider vinegar is also about 4–6 percent

and just right for most pickles but too strong for fruits or bland foods. Avoid using homemade vinegar as it may be unstable. Also avoid boiling for too long as this can change the pH of the vinegar solution. Never decrease the amount of vinegar specified if the pickles are too tart as this may change the pH of the pickles and, thus, their safety. One-quarter cup (2 oz/60 g) of sugar per 1 quart (1 l) of vinegar can be added safely.

A NOTE FOR READERS

The term "canning" is used in North America to mean preserving foods both in metal cans and in glass jars. Home preserving in metal cans is a rarity and "canning," in this book, means the process known in the UK and Australia as "bottling."

In the section on canning, both the processing of high-acid foods (fruits) at the temperature of boiling water and the processing of low-acid foods (vegetables) at higher temperatures, attainable only in a special pressure canner, are discussed. Home canning of low-acid foods is still widely practiced in North America, and is endorsed by the United States Department of Agriculture (USDA) and the corresponding Canadian government organizations, from which home canners can obtain detailed instructions and advice, either through USDA publications or from local agents, on this method. Without this kind of support (for example, to have the accuracy of the gauge on a pressure canner checked each year), home canning of low-acid foods is not recommended.

Discussion of pressure canners refers to quarts (q) of capacity, and recipes for pressure canning refer to pounds (lb) of pressure.

FREEZING FRUITS AND VEGETABLES

$\mathscr{H}$olding fruits and vegetables at 0°F (−18°C) does not kill micro-organisms that can spoil food, it simply stops the growth of microbes on a temporary basis. While a varying amount of bacteria is killed during freezing, the numbers killed are unpredictable and many survive. Frozen foods should be used within a reasonable time, since there is a gradual loss of quality. See the chart on pages 34–37 and the recipes in this chapter for maximum recommended storage times.

EQUIPMENT

Wide chest-type freezers are the most efficient to operate since cold air sinks. They are, however, less convenient to organize and require more floor space than the upright type. Upright freezers take up much less room, and many are self-defrosting. Self-defrosting freezers take more electricity to operate. Side-by-side or stacked refrigerator/freezers with separate controls work reasonably well. Allow space behind any unit for ventilation and select a dry, relatively cool location. The freezer temperature should be kept at 0°F (−18°C), or below, at all times. Set the temperature at −10°F (−23°C), and it will remain below 0°F (−18°C) when unfrozen food is added.

It is best to keep an inventory of what you have frozen. The simplest, most effective way is to have an inventory sheet taped on the freezer door, with accompanying pencil on a string to check each item in and out. Organizing this list by freezer shelf is a good idea. Make this a permanent routine. Always label packages clearly with the correct date and contents, using a proper freezer marker.

PACKAGING

Everything placed in your freezer should be protected by moisture-proof and vapor-proof material. The most convenient way to package frozen food is the pressure-locking, extra-heavy-gauge plastic bag. Thin plastic bags and plastic sheet wraps, even those that are marked "freezer," are usually moisture- but not vapor-proof, as they permit oxygen to pass through to some extent. Food should be overwrapped with heavy-duty aluminum foil or a heavy-gauge plastic bag, insuring that moisture cannot cross the wrapper barrier. The disadvantages of bags include awkward, space-consuming shapes and no ability to recycle them. To avoid awkward shapes, use a baking sheet to stack bags of newly packed food flat, or mold the bag into an empty milk carton. Rigid, wide-mouth freezer containers are expensive but they can be re-used, and their square shape saves valuable room. No matter what type of freezer packaging you choose, make certain that it is sealed tightly so that it is moisture- and vapor-proof.

> ### HEADSPACE
> *Since water (including the water present in all foods) expands when it freezes, freezer containers packed with food require headspace (room between the food and the lid) of ¹/₂ inch (1 cm) for wet and dry pack in the 1-pint (2-cup / 500-ml) size, and 1 inch (2.5 cm) for wet pack in the 4-cup (1-quart / 1-l) size.*

Vacuum Sealing Vacuum sealing fresh produce to be frozen (using a pump to withdraw air from bags so that they fit the contents closely), limits the amount of air that comes in contact with the produce, thereby reducing oxidation — one reason for food deteriorating in flavor or quality in the freezer. Follow the manufacturer's directions carefully. But remember that vacuum-sealed fruits and vegetables are not shelf stable and still need to be preserved.

Rigid containers should be filled as full as possible, allowing only room for headspace.

Most types of berry and other delicate fruits should be free-frozen (placed in a single layer on baking sheets and frozen for a couple of hours) to set their shape before vacuum sealing. Other fruits and vegetables can also be free-frozen for added convenience, then packed in bags or containers.

Safety Precautions After Freezing

Thaw frozen foods in the refrigerator rather than on the counter top so that organisms that thrive at room temperature cannot grow. You can also thaw food in a microwave oven on the defrost setting immediately before cooking and serving. Cook each type of vegetable separately, while still frozen, in small amounts of water in a covered saucepan or in a microwave oven. Frozen vegetables require only one-half to one-third of the cooking time needed for fresh vegetables. Corn on the cob is the only vegetable that should be thawed completely before it is cooked, for best flavor. Do not cook the corn in boiling water; instead, steam, or roast it in the oven.

Preparing Vegetables for Freezing

Make sure that you choose the best quality produce that is not overripe or bruised. All produce should be cleaned well, and equipment, counter top, and hands also should be clean.

Blanching is the most satisfactory way to prepare vegetables for freezing and is certainly worth the effort.

Because blanching inactivates enzymes that can cause unwanted texture, flavor, and color changes during storage, blanched vegetables keep longer and have better quality than unblanched ones. Blanched vegetables also retain more vitamins during storage.

BLANCHING VEGETABLES There are three ways to blanch vegetables:

Boiling Water — Easy. Place 1 lb (500 g) of vegetables in about 4 quarts (4 l) of briskly boiling water. Begin timing once the water comes to a boil again after adding the vegetables. While the water is boiling, gently agitate or stir the vegetables with a mixing spoon to insure even heat distribution.

Steam Blanching — Always wins the taste test. Place a steaming basket about 3–4 inches (8–10 cm) above the briskly boiling water. Place the vegetables in a single layer. Time from when you replace the lid.

Microwave Blanching — Is the simplest and the vegetable color remains more vivid. Follow the manufacturer's directions for the correct way to use your microwave oven.

Remember to add 30 seconds to the blanching time for each 500 feet (150 m) above sea level because at higher altitudes water comes to a boil at lower temperatures.

FREEZING ADVICE

❧ Freeze water in milk cartons and use blocks of ice in a bowl or sink to cool the vegetables after blanching. This works better than using ice cubes.

❧ An alternate method is to dunk the steaming basket of blanched vegetables into ice water for a few moments. Place in a single layer on clean dish towels to dry and pack immediately.

PREPARING FRUITS FOR FREEZING

DRY PACK Very simple — nothing is added to the fresh, clean fruit. Freeze berries and melon balls in single layers on baking sheets and, when frozen hard, store them in plastic bags. Serve fruit frozen by this method with the ice crystals still remaining so that the fruit holds its shape.

WET PACK Fruits store quite well in added liquid. Fruit juice, frozen concentrated orange or other concentrated juices, sugar syrup, water, or even more of the same fruit crushed can be used. Follow the recipes carefully. It takes about 1/2 cup (4 fl oz/ 125 ml) of cooled syrup for tightly packed fruits in 2-cup (1-pint/500-ml) containers and about 1 cup (8 fl oz/250 ml) for 4-cup (1-quart/1-l) containers.

Thin Sugar Syrup — 2 parts sugar to 4 parts water.

Medium Sugar Syrup — 3 parts sugar to 4 parts water. Very light and mild honey is an excellent choice for wet packs. You only need to reduce by half the amount of sweetener called for in the recipe.

Cooled Thin Syrup — 1 part honey to 2 parts water.

Cooled Medium Syrup — 2 parts honey to 2 parts water.

Some fruits turn dark when freezing and, to help prevent this, it is necessary to add ascorbic acid (vitamin C) or lemon juice, which adds a flavor of its own, to the recipe. There are also commercial mixtures of citric acid, L- or iso-ascorbic acid, and glucose available to reduce darkening. A good rule of thumb is that if the fruit darkens easily when fresh, it will certainly darken in the freezer. The obvious ones include apples, peaches, nectarines, pears, figs, and apricots.

FREEZING HERBS

Herbs that freeze well include basil, burnet, chives, comfrey, chervil, cilantro (fresh corian- der), sweet fennel, lovage, most mints, parsley, savory, and some thymes.

Equipment

*stainless steel saucepan
paper towels
chopping board
sharp knife
waxed (greaseproof) paper
label*

Ingredients

any of the herbs listed above, frozen while they are still in season, plentiful, and at the peak of quality

*Finished Quantity
1 part fresh=1 part frozen*

1 BLANCH Holding the stems, dip the herbs in boiling water, swishing them gently through the water. When the color brightens they are ready. This process takes only a few seconds.

2 DRAIN Place the herbs on clean paper towels by the bunch to cool.

3 PREPARE FOR FREEZING Then prepare the herbs to your liking by either removing stems, chopping, or simply leaving them whole.

4 PLACE ON PAPER When air-cooled and dry, lay the herbs out in single layers on waxed paper, then roll up and label.

5 FREEZE Store in the freezer for enjoyment all winter long. Break off as much as you want and use frozen. You may keep the herbs thawed in the refrigerator for a few days.

SWEET POTATO PUDDING

Fresh sweet potatoes from the garden prepared and frozen this way will become a family favorite. Make enough for two puddings — Christmas is only a month after Thanksgiving!

Equipment

ovenproof and freezerproof baking dish
large mixing bowl
serving spoon
label

Ingredients

3 cups (1 lb/500 g) cooked sweet potatoes, mashed

1 cup (8 oz/250 g) sugar

2 eggs, lightly beaten

1 teaspoon vanilla extract (essence)

¹/₄ cup (2 fl oz/60 ml) milk

1 cup (8 oz/250 g) butter

1 cup (6 oz/185 g) packed brown sugar

¹/₃ cup (1¹/₂ oz/45 g) all-purpose (plain) flour

1 cup (4 oz/125 g) chopped nuts, optional

Finished Quantity
5 cups (2 lb/1 kg)

1 **PREPARE SWEET POTATO BASE**
Grease a baking dish. Combine the sweet potatoes, sugar, eggs, vanilla, milk, and ¹/₂ cup (4 oz/125 g) of the butter. Place in the prepared baking dish.

2 **MAKE TOPPING** Melt the remaining ¹/₂ cup (4 oz/125 g) butter. Combine with the brown sugar, flour, and nuts.

3 **SPRINKLE ON TOPPING**
Cover the potatoes with the topping.

4 **FREEZE AND SERVE** Place the pudding in the freezer until needed. Thaw in the refrigerator. Preheat the oven to 350°F (180°C/Gas 4). Bake uncovered for 30 minutes, and serve.

FREEZING TIP

For easy freezer storage, it is a good idea to line a baking dish with aluminum foil before adding the food. Place the package in the freezer until the food is frozen hard. Remove the baking dish, and store the package in a labeled, dated plastic bag. To serve, simply remove the foil, return the food to the baking dish, then thaw in the refrigerator and reheat.

This elegant appetizer is a great choice for a summer buffet or picnic.

skillet (frying pan)
mixing spoon
serving spoon
freezer container
label

³/₄ cup (6 fl oz/185 ml) olive oil

2 eggplants (aubergines), peeled and cubed

1 clove garlic, chopped

3 sticks celery, chopped

2 medium onions, chopped

¹/₂ cup (2¹/₂ oz/75 g) green olives, finely chopped

1 cup (8 fl oz/250 ml) homemade or canned Italian tomato sauce

¹/₄ cup (1¹/₂ oz/45 g) capers

¹/₄ cup (2 fl oz/60 ml) white wine vinegar

1 tablespoon sugar

ℱinished 𝒬uantity
2¹/₂ cups (1¹/₄ lb/625 g)

1 **HEAT OIL. ADD EGGPLANT AND GARLIC** In a skillet, heat the oil and add the eggplant and garlic. Cook over moderately high heat for 8–10 minutes until lightly browned. Stir often.

2 **REMOVE EGGPLANT. ADD CELERY, ONIONS, AND OLIVES** Take out the eggplant and add the celery, onions, and olives. Cook until tender, about 5 minutes.

3 ADD TOMATO SAUCE
Stir in the tomato sauce and simmer for 5 minutes.

4 ADD EGGPLANT, CAPERS, VINEGAR, AND SUGAR
Mix in the eggplant, capers, vinegar, and sugar, and cook over low heat for 5 minutes.

5 TRANSFER TO A STORAGE CONTAINER
Spoon into a freezer container, seal, and label.

6 FREEZE
Place the container in the freezer. Store for up to 3 months. To serve, thaw in the refrigerator and serve cold or at room temperature.

VIDALIA ONION CASSEROLE

This recipe freezes well and can be enjoyed all year round.

Equipment

chopping board
sharp knife
skillet (frying pan)
mixing spoon
stainless steel saucepan
serving spoon
ovenproof and freezerproof
baking dishes
labels

Ingredients

5–6 large Vidalia (sweet salad) onions

¹/₃ cup (3 oz/90 g) butter

2 tablespoons all-purpose (plain) flour

1 teaspoon mustard powder

¹/₂ teaspoon pepper

1 cup (8 fl oz/250 ml) milk

¹/₂ cup (2 oz/60 g) grated cheddar cheese

1 cup (4 oz/125 g) bread crumbs

Finished Quantity
3 cups (1¹/₂ lb/750 g)

1 SLICE ONIONS Thinly slice the onions to equal 4–5 cups.

2 SAUTÉ ONIONS In a large skillet, melt 3 tablespoons (1¹/₂ oz/45 g) of the butter. Add the onions and sauté until soft, stirring occasionally. Remove from heat.

3 MAKE ROUX In a saucepan, melt 2 tablespoons (1 oz/30 g) of the remaining butter and stir in the flour, mustard, and pepper.

4 **ADD MILK AND CHEESE** Slowly stir in the milk and cheese. Cook until thickened.

5 **TRANSFER SAUCE AND ONIONS TO BAKING DISHES** Line the baking dishes with aluminum foil, if desired. Spoon alternate layers of the onions and sauce into the baking dishes.

6 **COVER WITH BREAD CRUMBS AND BUTTER** Sprinkle the top with the bread crumbs and dot with the remaining butter. Cover and freeze. If you have used a foil lining, freeze until the food is hard, then remove the baking dish, wrap the food, label, and freeze.

7 **SERVE** Remove the foil, if used, and return the food to the dish in which it was frozen. Thaw in the refrigerator. Bake for 15–20 minutes at 375°F (190°C/Gas 5), and serve.

PREPARATION TIPS

❧ The Vidalia (sweet salad) onion season is short and they don't last long in cold storage. This onion casserole recipe makes Vidalias available all year long.

❧ Remove frozen dishes from the freezer the day before they are required and transfer to the refrigerator to thaw.

Serve this soup in tea cups on saucers as part of a buffet.

Equipment

large mixing bowl
mixing spoon
ladle
freezer container
label

Ingredients

6 medium tomatoes, peeled, cored, and chopped

2 medium cucumbers, peeled, seeded, and chopped

1 large onion, chopped

1 quart (1 l) tomato juice

1 small green bell pepper (capsicum), chopped

1 stick celery, chopped

1 clove garlic, minced

1/2 teaspoon hot pepper sauce (such as Tabasco)

1/3 cup (3 fl oz/90 ml) red wine vinegar

2 tablespoons olive oil

Finished Quantity
1 1/2 quarts (1.5 l)

1 COMBINE INGREDIENTS In a bowl, combine all of the ingredients, stirring well.

2 TRANSFER TO FREEZER CONTAINER Ladle into a clean freezer container.

3 SEAL AND FREEZE Cover tightly and label. Place in the freezer for up to 3 months. Thaw in the refrigerator and serve chilled.

SERVING TIPS

❧ Garnished with a dollop of low-fat sour cream, this refreshing gazpacho is a low-calorie delight.

❧ The vegetables will be softer than fresh ones, so you may like to add some extra chopped fresh celery for texture when serving.

Avocado Purée

Use very ripe black-skinned California variety (Haas) avocados for this recipe. There will be no more waiting for a rock-hard green one to ripen on your counter top! Use as a dip, or thin with chicken stock for a cold soup.

Equipment

chopping board
sharp knife
large mixing bowl
fork
serving spoon
freezer container
label

Ingredients

3 very ripe avocados

6 teaspoons lemon juice

Finished Quantity
1¹/2 cups (12 oz / 375 g)

1 **PREPARE AVOCADOS** Halve, pit, peel, and mash the avocados quickly.

2 **ADD LEMON JUICE** Stir the lemon juice into the purée with a fork, to prevent the avocado discoloring.

3 **PLACE IN FREEZER CONTAINER** Pack the purée into a clean freezer container with a tight lid, leaving 1 inch (2.5 cm) headspace.

4 **SEAL AND FREEZE** Cover tightly, label, and place in the freezer for up to 2 months. Thaw in the refrigerator.

SUMMER SQUASH SOUP

Any squash or pumpkin can be used in this recipe but some of the tougher varieties have to be peeled, cut into chunks, and par-boiled first.

Equipment

skillet (frying pan)
mixing spoon
freezer containers
labels

Ingredients

1/2 cup (4 oz/125 g) butter

20–24 (2 1/4 lb/1.125 kg) small yellow summer (crookruck or straight) squash, sliced

1 clove garlic, minced

2 large onions, chopped

10 oz (315 g) broccoli, chopped

3–4 tablespoons all-purpose (plain) flour

2 cups (16 fl oz/500 ml) whole or skim milk

pinch of fresh thyme

2 cups (16 fl oz/500 ml) chicken stock

Finished Quantity
4 quarts (4 l)

1 **SAUTÉ SQUASH, GARLIC, AND ONIONS. ADD BROCCOLI** Melt the butter in a skillet, and sauté the squash, garlic, and onions until limp. Add the broccoli and cook until it is also soft and limp.

2 **MIX IN FLOUR, REMOVE FROM HEAT, THEN ADD MILK AND THYME** Mix in the flour, being careful not to let the mixture burn. When well combined and cooked slightly, remove from heat and gradually add the milk and thyme, mixing well.

3 **REHEAT, ADD STOCK, AND REDUCE SLIGHTLY** Return to heat and stir in the stock. Cook until thickened, then reduce heat to low and simmer for 5 minutes.

4 **PLACE IN FREEZER CONTAINERS, SEAL, AND FREEZE** Pack for the freezer in clean containers. Seal tightly, label, and place in the freezer for up to 2 months. To serve, thaw in the refrigerator and heat gently, stirring occasionally, or thaw and heat in a microwave oven.

OVEN-BAKED POTATOES

Developed by the Extension Service of Pennsylvania State University, this recipe has been embellished over the years by my family. I always make twice as much as we can eat at one meal, putting the remainder in the freezer.

Equipment

chopping board
sharp knife
large mixing bowl
clean dish towel
paper towels
baking sheet
basting brush
freezer container
label

Ingredients

2 lb (1 kg) large baking potatoes, peeled if desired

vegetable oil or coating spray (cooking spray)

olive oil

Finished Quantity
2 lb (1 kg)

1 **SLICE POTATOES** Cut the potatoes into uniform-sized strips. Long, large wedges are best.

2 **RINSE** Dip the potato strips in cold water.

3 **DRY** Turn out onto a dish towel and pat dry with absorbent paper towels.

4 **GREASE BAKING SHEET** Coat a baking sheet with vegetable oil using a brush or coating spray.

5 **ARRANGE POTATOES** Place the potatoes on the baking sheet in one layer and brush or spray with olive oil (keep a sprayer or mister container filled with olive oil for this use).

6 **BAKE, THEN COOL** Preheat the oven to 450°F (230°C/Gas 8). Bake in the oven on the lowest shelf until they brown, about 20–25 minutes, turning once or twice. Place in the refrigerator immediately to cool.

7 **PLACE IN FREEZER CONTAINER** When cool, transfer to a freezer container, label, and freeze. Keep the potatoes frozen for up to 1 month.

8 **SERVE** Spread the frozen potatoes on a baking sheet and bake at 450°F (230°C/Gas 8) until thawed and golden. Turn once or twice.

SERVING TIP

You may want to sprinkle oven-baked potatoes with some Parmesan cheese, garlic powder, or herb-flavored salt toward the end of baking for a deliciously different taste sensation.

APPLE-CRUMB PIE

You can have a dessert in an emergency if you keep one of these in the freezer.

Equipment

stainless steel saucepan
tongs
strainer
mixing bowl
pie dish
food processor
serving spoon

Ingredients

Apple Filling

12 oz (375 g) dried apples

1 quart (1 l) apple cider

3 tablespoons cornstarch (cornflour)

$^1/_4$ teaspoon ground nutmeg

$^1/_3$ cup (3 oz/90 g) sugar

9-inch (23-cm) shortcrust pastry pie shell

Crumb Mixture

$^1/_2$ cup (4 oz/125 g) sugar

$^3/_4$ cup (3 oz/90 g) all-purpose (plain) flour

$^1/_3$ cup (3 oz/90 g) butter

Finished Quantity
Serves 6

1 **COOK DRIED APPLES** In a saucepan, simmer the dried apples in the cider until soft but not broken, about 30 minutes.

2 **DRAIN AND COOL** Place the apples in a strainer and drain, reserving $^1/_4$ cup (2 fl oz/60 ml) of the liquid. Allow the apples to cool before proceeding.

3 **COMBINE APPLE FILLING INGREDIENTS** In a mixing bowl, combine the cornstarch, nutmeg, and sugar with the apples.

FREEZING FRUITS AND VEGETABLES

4 **ADD RESERVED LIQUID** Pour the reserved cooking liquid over the apple mixture and mix gently.

5 **PLACE IN PIE DISH** Transfer the filling to a 9-inch (23-cm) unbaked pie shell or leave it off and spoon it directly into a buttered 9-inch (23-cm) pie dish.

6 **MAKE CRUMB MIXTURE** In a food processor, combine the crumb mixture ingredients.

7 **SPREAD OVER APPLE FILLING AND FREEZE** Spoon the crumb mixture over the apple filling. The pie may be baked at this point, or frozen for up to 6 months.

8 **BAKE** Preheat the oven to 425°F (220°C/Gas 7). Bake the pie for about 1 hour, until golden brown.

9 **SERVE** Serve the pie with thick (double) cream, if desired.

Fruits, Vegetables	*Preparation for Freezing*	*Storage Time*
Apples	Peel, core, slice, toss with lemon juice; pack dry or mixed with a little honey.	1 year
Apricots	Dip in boiling water 15 seconds, then in cold water, and slip off skins. Halve, pit, pack in honey syrup or sugar syrup with lemon juice added.	1 year
Artichokes	Choose young artichokes. Cut off tops and trim to cone shape, removing ends of leaves. Wash, blanch 8 minutes or steam 10 minutes.	1 year
Asparagus	Use young stalks. Trim off ends, wash, and cut into lengths. Blanch 4 minutes or steam 5 minutes.	1 year
Avocados	Best frozen as a purée — see recipe page 27.	1 year
Bananas	Peel and mash or cut into chunks. Mix with lemon juice. Freeze chunks loose on baking sheet, then bag. Use before completely thawed.	1 year
Beans, green or yellow	Choose young beans, wash, drain, trim, or cut as desired. Blanch 3 minutes or steam 4 minutes.	1 year
Beans, lima	Choose young, bright green pods, wash. Blanch 2 minutes or steam 4 minutes, drain, shell, and rinse in cold water.	1 year
Beets (beetroot)	Use young and tender beets. Trim tops leaving $1/2$ inch (1 cm) of stems. If less than 2 inches (5 cm) in diameter, blanch 2–3 minutes; if larger, cook until tender. Chill, remove tops and skins, and pack whole, sliced, or diced.	1 year
Berries	Pick over. Wash, drain, freeze loose on a baking sheet, then bag.	1 year
Broccoli	Choose young, firm, green heads. Rinse, trim, peel stems, split into pieces no more than $1 1/2$ inches (4 cm) across. Soak in cold salted water 15 minutes; drain, blanch 3 minutes or steam 4 minutes.	1 year
Brussels sprouts	Use young, green sprouts. Rinse, trim, removing outer leaves, blanch 4 minutes or steam 6 minutes.	1 year
Cabbage	Trim, shred or cut into wedges. Blanch shredded cabbage $1 1/2$ minutes in boiling water or 2 minutes in steam; wedges, 3 minutes in boiling water or 4 minutes in steam.	1 year
Carrots	Use young carrots. Trim, wash, peel. Leave baby carrots whole, slice or dice larger ones. Blanch small pieces 2 minutes, larger pieces 3 minutes, whole carrots 5 minutes, or steam 1 minute longer.	1 year

Fruits, Vegetables	Preparation for Freezing	Storage Time
Cauliflower	Use firm, white cauliflower. Wash, break into florets. Soak in salted water 15 minutes, rinse, blanch 3 minutes or steam 5 minutes.	1 year
Celeriac	Wash, trim, slice, or cube. Blanch 4 minutes or steam 5 minutes.	1 year
Celery	Use young stalks. Clean, slice, blanch 3 minutes or steam 4 minutes. Frozen celery is suitable for use only in cooking.	1 year
Cherries	Wash, chill, stem, and pit. Toss with lemon juice to keep color.	1 year
Citrus fruit (grapefruit, lemons, limes, oranges)	Chill, peel, freeze in skin-on segments; or remove outer membrane when peeling, then cut out skinless segments. Pack dry, or freeze skinless segments loose on baking sheet, then bag.	4 months
Coconut	Pierce two of the eyes with a sharp instrument such as a skewer, drain juice, bake nut in hot oven 15 minutes. Lay hot nut down and hit center of shell to split it. Prize out flesh with a short, strong knife, and remove brown skin with a vegetable peeler. Chop or grate flesh, then bag.	1 year
Corn	Freeze as soon as possible after picking. Remove husk and silk, wash, blanch 6–8 minutes in boiling water or steam. Cool and freeze ears whole or cut off kernels and freeze.	1 year
Cranberries	Choose plump, glossy fruit. Sort, wash, drain; spread on paper towels to dry, pack dry.	1 year
Eggplant (aubergine)	Choose firm, heavy, glossy fruit. Wash and peel. Slice or dice, dip in solution of 1 tablespoon lemon juice to 1 quart (1 l) water. Blanch 4 minutes or steam 6 minutes, and dip again in lemon juice solution. Freeze with wrap between slices to separate for frying.	1 year
Figs	Wash, cut off stems, peel, cover with sugar syrup with lemon juice added, to prevent browning.	1 year
Garlic	Freeze unpeeled cloves; or peel and mince. Shape into a log, using plastic freezer wrap. Place in a closed glass jar, to prevent odor from transferring to other foods. When frozen, overwrap well or store in sealed container. Or place minced garlic in ice-cube trays, then cover with plastic freezer wrap. When frozen hard, pack in bags.	6 months

Fruits, Vegetables	Preparation for Freezing	Storage Time
Grape leaves	Choose large, tender, pale green leaves. Blanch by holding a few at a time in boiling water 2 minutes or until color dulls. Dip in cold water, pat dry with towels, pack in bags.	1 year
Grapes	Wash, stem, leave whole if seedless, or halve and seed. To use, dip one at a time, while still frozen, into lukewarm water, and skins will slip off.	1 year
Herbs	Wash, dip in boiling water a few seconds until color brightens, then cool in cold water. Remove stems, chop. Freeze on baking sheets and pack dry, or put into ice-cube trays, cover with water, and freeze, then bag.	1 year
Kiwi fruit	Choose ripe but firm fruits. Peel, slice, pack in sugar syrup.	1 year
Kohlrabi and rutabaga (swede)	Use young vegetables. Wash, trim, peel, slice, or dice. Blanch 3 minutes or steam 4 minutes.	1 year
Leeks	Use young, tender leeks. Wash well, trim off outer leaves, tops, and bases. Slice, freeze in bags for up to 9 months.	9 months –1 year
Melons	Choose fully ripe but firm fruit. Peel, seed, slice, cube, or ball. Pack in bags or containers, serve before completely thawed.	1 year
Mushrooms	Choose firm, tender mushrooms. Trim off ends of stems, slice larger mushrooms. Steam 3–4 minutes or sauté until almost cooked. Cool quickly and pack in bags. Frozen mushrooms can be added directly to recipes without thawing.	1 year
Nectarines and peaches	Choose ripe fruit. Wash, peel, halve, pit, and slice into sugar syrup with $1/2$ teaspoon each L-ascorbic acid (vitamin C) and citric acid added for each quart (liter) of syrup. Pack into containers, or freeze whole. To use, put fruit, still frozen, in strainer and pour boiling water over until the skins crack, then pull off the skins.	1 year
Okra	Choose young, tender pods. Wash and remove stems without rupturing the seed cells. Blanch 3 minutes or steam 5 minutes. Freeze whole or sliced.	1 year
Onions	Peel and slice or dice. It is better to use onions, unblanched, within 6 months. Pack in containers, or overwrap bags, to prevent odor from transferring to other foods in freezer.	6 months

Fruits, Vegetables	Preparation for Freezing	Storage Time
Parsnips	Choose young parsnips. Trim, wash, peel, and slice or cube. Blanch 3 minutes or steam 5 minutes.	1 year
Pears	Choose firm, full-flavored, juicy pears. Wash, peel, core, and blanch 2 minutes in sugar syrup, then drain, cool, and pack in cooled syrup with lemon juice added.	1 year
Peas	Wash, shell, and blanch 2 minutes or steam 3 minutes.	1 year
Peppers, bell (capsicums) and chilies	Choose firm peppers with glossy skins. Wash, halve, and remove seeds and ribs, and freeze. Peppers lose their crispness when frozen.	1 year
Pineapple	Peel, trim, core, and slice or cut in wedges. Pack in its own juice or sugar syrup.	1 year
Plums	Choose firm, ripe fruit. Wash, halve, pit, and pack in bags; or pack in sugar syrup; or cover with sugar, stand until sugar dissolves, and pack in this juice.	1 year
Pumpkin (winter squash)	Wash and chop. Remove seeds. Boil, steam, or oil and bake at 375°F (190°C/Gas 5), until soft. Cool, peel, and mash. Freeze in containers.	2 months
Rhubarb	Choose tender, red stalks. Trim off leaves and ends, wash, cut into short lengths, blanch $1^1/_2$ minutes.	1 year
Spinach and other leafy greens	Choose young, tender leaves. Wash well, trim off stems and heavy midribs. Blanch 2 minutes or steam 3 minutes. Chop if desired. Cool, press, and freeze.	1 year
Tomatoes	Drop into boiling water for 30 seconds, then into cold water. Remove skins. Quarter or purée; or freeze whole, unpeeled on baking sheets, then bag. When wanted, run, still frozen, under warm water and skins will slip off. Frozen tomatoes are suitable only for cooking.	1 year
Turnips	Choose young turnips. Cut off tops, wash, peel, and slice or cube. Blanch $2^1/_2$ minutes.	1 year
Zucchini (courgettes) and summer (pattypan) squash	Wash, slice, blanch in steam 2 minutes. Zucchini and summer squash that have been frozen are watery when thawed. They are best reheated when still frozen.	1 year

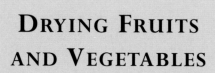

DRYING FRUITS AND VEGETABLES

$\mathcal{D}$ry food has the moisture removed and can't support the growth of micro-organisms. Properly dried food retains most nutrients as well as flavor and color. Use only food in fresh, prime condition and work quickly.

PREPARATION FOR DRYING

Food to be dried should be cut into small or thin pieces so that it will dry quickly. Pieces to be dried together should be of about the same size so that they will take the same amount of time to dry.

Most fruits need no preparation for drying beyond washing, slicing, or cutting up, but vegetables need blanching first to set the color. Blanching hastens drying by softening the tissues, checking the ripening process, as well as destroying enzymes to prevent undesirable changes in texture, flavor, and color during drying or storage. Steam blanching and microwave blanching are the best methods because blanching in boiling water adds more liquid to the food initially, thereby making the drying process longer. Steam- or microwave-blanched vegetables will hold up to taste tests much better as well. There is no need to cool the food afterward, as for freezing. Just put the vegetables directly onto drying trays. For

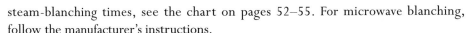

steam-blanching times, see the chart on pages 52–55. For microwave blanching, follow the manufacturer's instructions.

In commercial drying operations, apricots, apples, pears, and peaches are often pre-sulfured for drying. Sulfuring preserves the color and vitamin C content and prevents oxidized flavor. However, it may adversely affect asthmatics or people who suffer from allergies. Sulfuring of light-colored fruits for sun-drying is recommended. Another way to retain the color, although this is only partially effective, is to dip the fruit in unsweetened lemon or pineapple juice, or ascorbic acid (vitamin C) solution (1,500 mg vitamin C dissolved in 1 quart [1 l] of cold water).

METHODS OF DRYING

SUN-DRYING The key to sun-drying is air movement. Weather is everything, and the drier and warmer the air the better. Simple techniques and equipment are the best. Picture frames or fruit crates with clean old sheets stapled over the outside of the frame are a good choice for frame making, but don't use green wood, that tends to warp, or pine, that has annoying resin, to make your frame. In days gone by, many people used their window screens. Make these frames so that they can fit into your oven. Cake-cooling racks are a good choice when making small quantities.

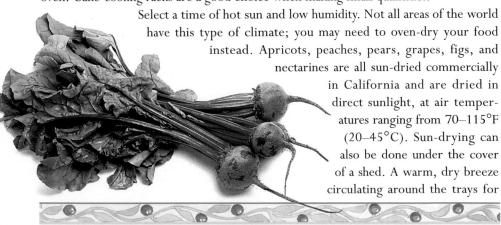

Select a time of hot sun and low humidity. Not all areas of the world have this type of climate; you may need to oven-dry your food instead. Apricots, peaches, pears, grapes, figs, and nectarines are all sun-dried commercially in California and are dried in direct sunlight, at air temperatures ranging from 70–115°F (20–45°C). Sun-drying can also be done under the cover of a shed. A warm, dry breeze circulating around the trays for

2 days is ideal. Place the food in a single layer on a tray or rack, skin-side down, so that the moister side will have dried out enough not to stick to the tray. Take the trays in at night to avoid dew. Damp air may make the food go moldy. If there are insects around, cover the trays with cheesecloth (muslin), insuring that the material is not touching the food.

OVEN-DRYING A temperature exceeding 140°F (60°C) is too high because the food may cook on the outside, forming a skin that traps moisture inside. Set the oven to 140°F (60°C). Many ovens cannot be set as low as this, so set it as low as possible, using an oven thermometer to check the temperature inside, and experiment with how much to leave the door open to keep the temperature at 100–140°F (40–60°C). Add the food on trays or racks as for sun-drying, or place it directly on the oven racks; keep the oven door propped open with a spoon and leave for 12–14 hours; overnight is ideal. Don't overload the oven with food. Check the trays, changing their positions, from time to time.

PASTEURIZING AND STORING

When dried food is done, vegetables will be crisp, maybe even leather-like; dried fruits will be tough or pliable. Some fruits will be sticky (see the drying chart on pages 52–55). Foods still warm directly from the drying source will be softer. Allow to cool and then test for dryness.

Treat open-air-dried fruits and vegetables before storing in containers. Use your oven preheated to 175°F (80°C). Spread out the food on trays in a loose fashion not more than 1 inch (2.5 cm) deep. Heat for 10–15 minutes. Remove each batch and cool completely on clean dish towels. This will increase storage time by insuring that the food is thoroughly dry and by killing any insects (this includes checking for eggs, larvae, and adults it may have picked up outdoors). Your freezer can treat open-air-dried food too: Place the food in plastic freezer bags and hold below 0°F (–18°C) for at least 4 days. Freezing destroys fewer vitamins than the oven method, although it

cannot be done in a freezer/refrigerator with no separate door for a freezing unit because the food cannot be held at a low enough temperature.

Airtight glass jars are the best containers for dried food. Always store them in a dark, cool place. Containers should be full so that there is as little air in the jar as possible. Be sure to label and date each jar well.

Rehydrating (Reconstituting)

Put dried fruits or vegetables in the bottom of a saucepan and pour over just enough boiling water to cover the food. Cover the saucepan and leave on very low heat until the water is absorbed. The dried food will look and taste very similar to the fresh version. There are some exceptions to this general rule for reconstituting dried fruits and vegetables, and these are noted under individual entries in the drying chart on pages 52–55. Vegetables that are to be added to soups and stews need not be rehydrated first — just add them dry to the liquid in the recipe.

OVEN-DRIED APRICOTS

Apricots, peaches, pears, and grapes are great for oven-drying.

ℰquipment

*drying frame or oven rack
oven thermometer
storage jar
label*

ℐngredients

apricots (or any other food suitable for oven-drying), with stones removed

*ℱinished Quantity
1 part fresh = ¹/₃ part dried*

1 LAYER APRICOTS ON RACK Carefully place the apricots on the rack in a single layer.

2 PLACE IN OVEN Heat the oven to 140°F (60°C), add the rack and dry, leaving the oven door propped open with a mixing spoon, for 12–14 hours. Use an oven thermometer to check that the temperature stays at 140°F (60°C).

3 STORE Place the dried apricots in a clean, airtight, labeled jar, and store.

SUN-DRIED HERBS

Herbs such as thyme, rosemary, oregano, and tarragon sun-dry well.

ℰquipment

drying frame

ℐngredients

fresh herbs (or any other food suitable for sun-drying)

*ℱinished Quantity
1 part fresh = ¹/₂ part dried*

1 PLACE HERBS ON FRAME Spread the herbs on a drying frame in a covered, warm, dry, and airy place. Leave for 1–2 days, turning the herbs occasionally.

2 STORE The dried herbs are ready for storing.

SUN-DRYING TIP

Easy to sun-dry fruits include apples, apricots, cherries, dates, figs, grapes, guavas, nectarines, peaches, pears, and plums. Easy to sun-dry vegetables, which have been blanched, are mature shelled beans and peas, lentils, and soybeans.

LEATHER BRITCHES

No-one can be sure why the colonial settlers called strung dried beans and pea pods "leather britches." Perhaps it was because of the weathered and pliable end product. Give to friends for gifts, or enjoy seeing them hanging in your own kitchen.

Equipment

darning or trussing needle
heavy thread
stainless steel saucepan

Ingredients

about 6 cups (2 lb / 1 kg)
green or yellow beans or
pea pods

PREPARATION TIP
If using green beans, do not dry in direct sunlight as they will lose all color.

Finished Quantity
1 part fresh = ¹/2 part dried

1 STRING BEANS OR PEAS
Pierce the beans or peas about one-third of the way from one end with the needle, then string them on clean heavy thread.

2 BLANCH Steam-blanch the beans or peas, string and all, for about 6 minutes, or until pliable and bright green in color. Blot dry with a clean dish towel.

3 DRY Hang to dry in a warm, well-ventilated place.

4 STORE Hang under the eaves of the house, from the attic rafter, on a porch, or in your kitchen, if conditions permit.

Attractive paper bags and colorful yarn or string may be used if you wish to give these dried herbs as gifts. Another great idea is to cut decorative patterns into the paper bags.

Equipment

paper bags
rubber bands, yarn, or string
labels

Ingredients

clean, dry, fresh herb branches, sprigs, or leaves

Finished Quantity
1 part fresh = ¹/₂ part dried

1 **PLACE HERBS IN PAPER BAGS**
Gather stems and invert in paper bags in which you have punched multiple holes for air circulation.

2 **SECURE BAGS** Gather the bag tops around the stems and secure with rubber bands, yarn, or string.

3 **STORE** Line the bags on a shelf, label each bag, and you have an attractive line of aromatic riches for the winter. These make great, unique gifts presented dried in the paper bag and attractively labeled. Adding a bow in a festive color will enhance the gesture.

PREPARATION TIPS

🌿 *Try using the paper-bag method for drying basil, oregano, parsley, rosemary, tarragon, and thyme.*
🌿 *Don't crush the herbs until you are ready to use them so that you release the oils and flavors into your recipe, not the storage bags or your hands.*

These tomatoes make an ideal gift. The oil is delicious when poured over pasta or used for sautéeing vegetables.

Equipment

chopping board
sharp knife
plastic or stainless steel
window screens
cheesecloth (muslin)
baking sheet
storage jars
mixing bowl
paper towels
tongs
labels

Ingredients

30 ripe tomatoes

equal parts water and white wine vinegar, to cover

1 clove fresh garlic, minced

2 bay leaves

6 black peppercorns

1 tablespoon pine nuts

1 small dried red chili, crumbled

$^1/_2$ cup (4 fl oz / 125 ml) virgin olive oil

Finished Quantity
about 2 cups (10 oz / 315 g)

1 PREPARE TOMATOES Slice the tomatoes in half lengthwise.

2 ARRANGE TOMATOES ON SCREENS Put the tomatoes cut-side up on window screens covered with cheesecloth in a sunny location. Bring inside at night. After about 4 days the fruit will be leathery and pliable.

3 PASTEURIZE Freeze the tomatoes for 4 days below 0°F (−18°C) or heat them in the oven on a baking sheet for 10–15 minutes at 160°F (70°C) to destroy insects.

4 STORE Place the dried tomatoes in airtight glass jars and store in a cool, dark place — the refrigerator is ideal — for up to 6 months.

5 RECONSTITUTE
In a mixing bowl, soak the tomatoes in equal parts of water and vinegar and let stand for about 15 minutes, or until soft and chewy.

6 DRAIN Drain on paper towels and pat dry.

8 ADD MARINADE INGREDIENTS
Combine the marinade ingredients and pour over the tomatoes.

7 TRANSFER TO JARS
Pack into clean storage jars using tongs.

9 SEAL AND STORE
Clean the rims, cap tightly, and label. Let the flavors marry for about 1 week before using. Store in the refrigerator for up to 1 month after opening.

DRIED APPLE RINGS

These make a great snack to take hiking or camping, or for children to take to school. Reconstituted and patted dry on absorbent paper towels, they're ready for frying with pork chops or sausages.

Equipment

apple corer
chopping board
sharp knife
12-inch (30-cm) wooden
skewers, soaked in water
overnight
oven rack
storage container
label

Ingredients

12 firm but ripe apples,
peeled

2 tablespoons salt

1¹/₂ cups (12 fl oz / 375 ml)
water

Finished Quantity
3 cups (6¹/₂ oz / 200 g)

1 **PREPARE APPLES** Core the apples, slice into 1-inch (2.5-cm) thick rings, and soak for 10 minutes in the salt and water solution.

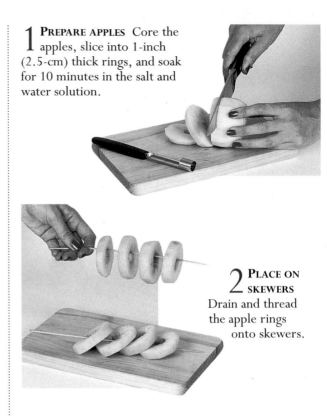

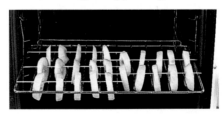

2 **PLACE ON SKEWERS** Drain and thread the apple rings onto skewers.

3 **BAKE** Place in a preheated 140°F (60°C) oven, alternating the apple rings on the rungs of the oven racks so that they are not touching. Bake for 4–5 hours or until leathery but pliable.

4 **COOL AND STORE** Let cool for 10–12 hours on dish towels. Place in a labeled airtight container in a cool, dark place. Soak for 24 hours in water to reconstitute.

If you don't have the right conditions for sun-drying herbs, they can be done just as well in the oven.

*baking sheet
mixing spoon
storage container
label*

clean, dry, fresh herb branches, sprigs, or leaves

*Finished Quantity
1 part fresh = ¹/₂ part dried*

1 ARRANGE HERBS ON BAKING SHEET Spread the clean, dry herbs evenly in one layer on a baking sheet.

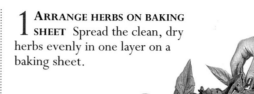

2 BAKE Place the herbs in a preheated 140°F (60°C) oven for about 45 minutes.

3 PROP OVEN DOOR OPEN Put a spoon in the oven door to prop open slightly for the last 15 minutes. Remove from the oven and stand for 12 hours, or overnight.

4 STORE Place the whole branches, sprigs, or leaves in a labeled airtight container. Keep for up to 6 months in a cool, dark place.

OVEN-DRYING TIP
Oven-drying is a more exact method than sun-drying; the only problem can be in keeping your oven at the correct, low temperature. Your aim in drying is not to heat the food, but rather to remove the moisture from it.

OVEN-DRIED TOMATOES

No peeling is required for this easy but elegant version of "Tuscan" dried tomatoes.

Equipment

chopping board
sharp knife
oven racks
mixing spoon
storage jars
labels

Ingredients

30 tomatoes

salt (optional)

1 PREPARE TOMATOES Halve the tomatoes lengthwise. Salt lightly, if desired.

2 PLACE ON OVEN RACKS Arrange the tomato slices, cut-side down, directly on the oven racks.

3 BAKE Set the oven to 140°F (60°C). Place the tomatoes in the oven for about 12–14 hours. This is good to do at night. Prop the oven door open with a spoon for the last hour to let moisture escape if the tomatoes are not dried completely.

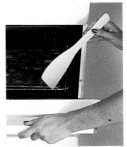

4 STORE Transfer the tomatoes to airtight jars, cover tightly, and label. Store in a cool, dark place for up to 6 months. Refrigerate upon opening and keep for 1 month.

PREPARATION TIPS

🌿 *Snip off the stem end of the tomato. You will see evidence of a pattern of seeds and pulp. Slice the tomato from end to end in the opposing direction to the way the seeds run so that you have two perfect halves with the seeds exposed. You can then remove the seeds easily with your thumb.*

🌿 *A sheet of aluminum foil in the bottom of your oven can be helpful for cleaning up after oven-drying foods.*

Finished Quantity
1 part fresh = ¹/4 part dried

AIR-DRIED MUSHROOMS

Most vegetables preserve best when blanched first, but mushrooms may be successfully dried without blanching. Always check with a local expert about wild mushrooms! If you can learn to recognize just one or two wild types, you will discover an untapped gold mine of enjoyment.

Equipment

chopping board
sharp knife
damp cloth
darning or trussing needle
strong thread
baking sheet
storage jars
labels

Ingredients

wild or domestic
(cultivated) mushrooms

1 PREPARE AND STRING MUSHROOMS Remove the stems of the mushrooms, if desired, or leave whole. Wipe with a damp cloth. Using a needle, string the mushrooms on strong thread.

2 DRY Hang the strings of mushrooms in the sun, for several days, until dry and almost brittle. Bring in at night. A good breeze helps.

3 BAKE Heat in a 160°F (70°C) oven on a baking sheet for 30 minutes to destroy insects.

4 STORE Place in clean jars. Cover and label. Store in a cool, dry place for 6 months. To reconstitute, soak for 30 minutes in warm water.

Finished Quantity
1 part fresh = 1/3 part dried

Fruits, Vegetables	Preparation for Drying	Dried Texture
Apples	Peel if desired, core, cut into slices or rings, dip in ascorbic acid solution. Blanch 4 minutes.	Pliable, slightly tough
Apricots	Halve and pit. Dip in ascorbic acid solution. Blanch 4 minutes.	Soft, pliable
Asparagus	Use only top 3 inches (8 cm) of spears. Blanch about 5 minutes, until tender and firm. When reconstituted, tips become tender and plumped, but stems are tough.	Very tough to brittle
Bananas	Peel, slice thinly, dip in ascorbic acid solution. Do not reconstitute, use dry as a snack only.	Pliable, chewy
Beans, green and yellow	Trim, cut on the diagonal into short lengths. Blanch 5 minutes. Alternately, beans can be dried on the stalk or by stringing the whole beans—see page 44.	Crisp, brittle
Beans, lima	Shell, blanch 5 minutes. To reconstitute, soak in cool water (1 cup [6 oz/185 g] beans to 2 cups [16 fl oz/500 ml] water) for 2 hours. Also can be dried on the stalk.	Hard, brittle
Beets (beetroot)	Trim tops, leaving 1/2 inch (1 cm) of stem. Blanch 45 minutes or until cooked through. Cool, remove tops and skin, slice thinly or dice.	Tough to brittle
Blueberries	Stem, blanch 1–2 minutes, then plunge into cold water to crack skins; or omit blanching and make a few nicks in skins with a sharp knife, so that moisture can escape easily.	Leathery, pliable
Broccoli	Trim, slice 1/2 inch (1 cm) thick. Blanch 4 minutes.	Crisp, brittle
Cabbage	Slice thinly. Blanch 2–3 minutes.	Brittle
Carrots	Wash, slice thinly. Blanch 2–3 minutes.	Tough to brittle
Cauliflower	Use florets only. Split stems, blanch 3 minutes.	Crisp, slightly browned
Celery	Trim off leaves, slice stalks in small pieces. Blanch 1 minute.	Brittle
Cherries	Stem, halve, and pit. Blanch 1 minute.	Leathery, pliable
Citrus peel	Peel fruit thinly, or grate skin, to obtain yellow or orange part only. Use dry.	Crisp

Fruits, Vegetables	Preparation for Drying	Dried Texture
Coconut	Pierce two of the eyes with a sharp instrument such as a skewer, drain juice, bake nut in a hot oven 15 minutes. Lay hot nut down and hit center of shell with a hammer to split it. Prize out the flesh with a short, strong knife or instrument such as a screwdriver, and remove brown skin with a vegetable peeler. Grate flesh or take off in thin slices with a vegetable peeler. Use dry.	Leathery to crisp
Corn	Remove husks and silk, blanch whole cobs 10 minutes, cut off kernels or dry whole.	Dry, brittle
Cucumber	Peel, slice, and blanch 1 minute.	Crisp
Dates	No treatment needed.	Leathery, deep russet or golden color
Eggplant (aubergine)	Peel, cut in 1/2-inch (1-cm) slices. Blanch 4 minutes.	Leathery to brittle
Figs	Halve.	Leathery
Garlic	Peel and slice thinly. Use dry.	Crisp
Grapes	Stem, crack skins by blanching 1–2 minutes, then plunging into cold water; or omit blanching and make a few nicks in the skins with a sharp knife or skewer, to let all of the moisture escape easily. Seedless grapes do not need to be treated before drying. Raisins cannot be reconstituted to grapes.	Wrinkled, soft (raisins)
Horseradish	Trim tops off, grate or slice. Use dry. Loses most of flavor on drying.	Brittle
Mushrooms	Wipe with a damp cloth, cut off stems if tough, slice 1/4 inch (0.5 cm) thick. Blanch 3 minutes. Can also be dried whole and without blanching.	Leathery to crisp
Nectarines and peaches	Halve and pit, dipping each half into ascorbic solution.	Soft, pliable, leathery
Okra	Cut off tips, slice, blanch 5 minutes.	Tough to brittle
Onions and leeks	Peel onions, trim leeks, and slice.	Brittle
Papaya (pawpaw)	Seed, peel, and slice.	Leathery to crisp

Fruits, Vegetables	Preparation for Drying	Dried Texture
Parsnip	Trim off tops, peel, dice, and blanch 5 minutes.	Tough to brittle
Pears	Halve and core, dipping each half into ascorbic acid solution.	Soft, pliable, leathery
Peas	Shell, blanch 3 minutes. To reconstitute, simmer covered, 30 minutes in 2 cups (16 fl oz/500 ml) of water to each cup of peas.	Wrinkled, hard, brittle
Peppers, bell (capsicums) and chilies	Halve bell peppers, remove seeds and ribs, slice into thin strips. Thread chilies together through the thickest part of stems and hang in a sunny, airy place. Leave hanging and use as needed.	Leathery to brittle Dark, shrunken, wrinkled, leathery
Pineapple	Peel, core, and slice. Blanch 1 minute.	Leathery, no longer sticky
Plums	Halve and pit.	Pliable, wrinkled, leathery (prunes)
Potatoes	Peel if desired, wash, slice 1/4 inch (0.5 cm) thick. Blanch 5 minutes, soak 45 minutes in 8 cups (2 q/2 l) water to 1/2 cup (4 fl oz/125 ml) lemon juice to prevent browning.	Brittle
Potatoes, sweet	Peel if desired, grate, slice, or dice. Blanch 3 minutes.	Tough to brittle
Pumpkin (winter squash)	Peel, seed, cut into thin slices. Blanch 3 minutes.	Tough to brittle
Rhubarb	Trim off leaves, cut stems on the diagonal into short pieces. Blanch 3 minutes.	Tough to crisp
Spinach and Swiss chard (silverbeet)	Cut into wide strips. Blanch 2 minutes.	Crisp, easily crumbled
Strawberries	Hull, halve or quarter. Blanch 1 minute.	Pliable, leathery
Tomatoes	Use paste-type tomatoes. Halve lengthwise or cut in thirds if very large.	Pliable, leathery

Fruits, Vegetables	Preparation for Drying	Dried Texture
Turnips	Trim off tops and roots, slice. Blanch 5 minutes.	Tough to brittle
Zucchini (courgettes) and summer (pattypan) squash	Slice thinly, sprinkle with seasoned salt.	Leathery to brittle

Note: *Some foods to be dried should be blanched either in boiling water or by steaming. Details of ascorbic acid solution are given on page 40. General directions for rehydrating (reconstituting) dried fruit and vegetables are given on page 42. Exceptions to these general directions are noted under individual entries above. Fruits can be eaten dried, as snacks.*

Lettuce and radish are not recommended for drying, and other vegetables sometimes eaten raw, such as celery and cucumber, will be suitable only for cooking when reconstituted. Brussels sprouts are not recommended for drying. Blueberries and strawberries dry successfully, but blackberries and raspberries are not recommended for drying.

CANNING FRUITS AND VEGETABLES

*C*anning preserves food by heating it in sealed containers. The heat destroys the micro-organisms (bacteria, yeasts, and molds) that grow in the food being canned. Air is driven from the container. As the jar cools and the contents contract, a partial vacuum is formed inside and the lid is pulled tightly onto the container so that it seals, preventing air and micro-organisms from entering. Home canning in metal cans is no longer common — nor is it advisable. This book deals only with canning in glass jars.

There are two kinds of canning. Hot-water canning, in which food, packed in jars, is processed in a hot-water bath; and pressure canning, in which food, packed in jars, is processed at temperatures above the boiling point of water (240–250°F/120–130°C). This is a procedure that can only be carried out in a specialized pressure canner.

It is important for safety to understand which foods should be processed by which method. If even a few potentially dangerous bacteria survive the canning process, they can multiply and cause food poisoning. The most dangerous of all, *Clostridium botulinum*, which causes the poisoning called botulism, can grow only in the absence of air, such as in a sealed canning jar.

While most bacteria, yeasts, and molds are easily destroyed by heat at temperatures below the boiling point of water, bacterial spores are much more difficult to destroy. In acid foods, where acidity prevents the growth of spore-forming bacteria, other bacteria can be destroyed at temperatures above 150°F (65°C). In low-acid foods, spores can be destroyed only at the higher temperatures attainable in a pressure canner.

Acidity is measured on a pH scale which runs from 0 to 14 — the lower the pH value, the more acid the food. Foods which have a pH at or below 4.6 are classified as acid and can be safely processed by boiling-water canning. Foods with a pH above 4.6 are classified as low-acid and must be processed by pressure canning. Most fruits are classified as acid; vegetables, meat, and fish are classified as low-acid foods. It is safe to prepare pickled vegetables by the hot-water method because the large amount of vinegar added will lower the pH to a point where "acid food" conditions prevail.

RECOMMENDATIONS FOR HOME CANNING OF TOMATOES

Acidification of whole, peeled tomatoes, halved, or quartered tomatoes, and tomato juice is done to improve flavor and more easily control spoilage by bacteria. The spores of these spoilage bacteria are destroyed in tomatoes without added acid in 1 minute at 190°F (90°C). They will not grow in tomatoes at pH 4.3 or below. It is not done to control growth of *Clostridium botulinum*, which will not grow in tomatoes unless the pH is 5.0 or above. Values of pH above 4.8 occur as a result of mold growth or the growth of bacteria, which require oxygen. Such growth is a result of failure to seal or of faulty seals on jars.

One teaspoon of lemon juice or vinegar should be added per pint (500 ml) of tomatoes. The tomatoes should then be processed in a gently boiling water bath for 45 minutes for a raw pack and 30 minutes for a hot pack. There is no problem with botulism in canned tomatoes if the jars are properly sealed and do not also contain meat or large amounts of low-acid vegetables, such as onions, celery, carrots, and bell peppers (capsicums), in stewed or spiced tomatoes.

SPECIAL TREATMENT FOR SOME HOT-CLIMATE FRUITS

Hot-climate fruits such as bananas, papaya (pawpaw), mango, melon, and figs are lower in acid than most cooler-climate fruits, and should similarly have their acidity increased before canning, alone or with other foods, by the hot-water method. To each 1-quart (1-l) hot-water pack, add 1/4 teaspoon of citric acid or 1 tablespoon of fresh lemon juice.

Safety Points

Microwave and oven canning are not recommended as they increase spoilage possibilities. For safe pressure canning, it is imperative to employ the use of a specially designed canner — don't try to do it in an ordinary pressure cooker. Open-kettle canning (boiling food in one large batch, then ladling it into sterilized jars), also called hot fill and hold, is acceptable only for pickled foods with pH values less than 4.0 and for jams and jellies.

A traditional precaution when using home-canned low-acid food is to boil it for 10 minutes (plus 1 additional minute per 1,000 feet [300 m] above sea level) before eating. USDA (and the corresponding Canadian) guidelines now say that low-acid foods that have been canned according to endorsed recommendations, and that meet all the above checkpoints, may be eaten without boiling.

> ### *Checkpoints*
>
> *1 The food was processed in a pressure canner.*
> *2 The gauge of the pressure canner was accurate (some canners have weighted controls that need to be checked regularly).*
> *3 Process times and temperatures were used for the size jar, style of pack, and food canned.*
> *4 The process time and pressure recommended for processing the food at your altitude were correct.*
> *5 The jar lid is firmly sealed and concave.*
> *6 Nothing has leaked from the jar.*
> *7 No liquid spurts out when the jar is opened.*
> *8 No unnatural or "off" odors can be detected.*

Equipment

All equipment must be clean. Essential items include a jar lifter, wide-mouth funnel, rack for the bottom of the canner, timer, and clean canning jars with two-piece lids: a metal vacuum lid and metal screw band. Mason-type jars with two-piece lids are the only canning jars recommended. You will also need a 21–23-quart (21–23-l) hot-water canner with a lid and jar rack, or a 16–22-quart (16–22-l) aluminum pressure canner with an accurate gauge and bottom rack (not a pressure cooker). Other equipment needed should be found in a well-stocked kitchen.

All canning containers must be tall enough to allow water to cover the jars. Filled jars displace water and cause the water level to rise even before boiling begins.

Before every use, wash the empty jars in hot water with detergent, rinsing very

thoroughly. Keep the clean jars and lids ready for use submerged in hot water or in an oven at 180°F (80°C).

LIDS Buy only the quantity of lids that you will use in 1 year. Self-sealing lids consist of two parts: a flat-metal lid, crimped around its bottom edge to form a trough which is filled with a colored gasket compound, and a metal screw band to hold the flat lid in place during processing. When the jars are processed, the gasket compound softens slightly and flows to cover the jar sealing surface, yet allows air to escape. As the jar cools and its contents contract, the lid is pulled firmly onto the jar and the gasket compound forms an airtight seal. The screw band should be gently removed after 24 hours as it will become difficult to remove, may rust, and may not work properly again. Washed, dried, and stored in a dry area, screw bands may be used many times. Flat lids can be used only once.

TESTING JAR SEALS After cooling the jars for 24 hours and removing the screw bands, test to see that the lids are properly sealed. You can do this by using one or more of the following options:

1 Press the middle of the lid with a finger. If it gives, then springs back when you release your finger, the lid is unsealed.

2 Tap the lid with the bottom of a teaspoon. If food is in contact with the underside of the lid, the jar is not sealed and will make a dull sound. A jar that is sealed correctly, with a vacuum under the lid, will make a ringing high-pitched sound.

3 Hold the jar at eye level and look across the lid. It should be concave (curved down slightly in the center) because it has been pulled down when the vacuum formed.

If a jar is found not to be sealed properly, remove the lid and check the jar's sealing surface for tiny nicks. If necessary, change the jar, add a new lid, and reprocess the jar within 24 hours. Alternatively, place this particular jar in the refrigerator and use every bit of the food within a few days.

PROCEDURES FOR CANNING

HOT PACK For hot packing, food is simmered first, then transferred, hot, to canning jars for processing.

Hot pack can be used for hot-water canning, as it helps to remove air from food tissues, shrinks food, helps keep the food from floating in the jars, and increases the

vacuum in sealed jars. At first, raw-packed foods may look better, but within a short storage period, the color and flavor of hot-packed foods will be superior.

Hot-pack liquid for fruits can be sweet syrup, juice made from some of the original food to be canned, purchased juice such as orange or apple, or water. A simple syrup of 2 cups (16 fl oz/500 ml) honey or 2 cups (16 oz/500 g) sugar and 1 quart (1 l) hot water works well. Do not use artificial sweeteners for canning as they lose their sweetness and develop an unpleasant taste at higher temperatures.

RAW PACK After a fairly tight pack, pour hot or cold liquid over the raw food. Any of the liquids mentioned in the hot-pack section can be used. Raw packing is suitable for vegetables to be processed in a pressure canner.

STORAGE AND LABELING

Completed vegetables and fruits must always be stored in a dry, dark, cool area. Lids corrode in damp atmospheres; loss of food color occurs from too strong light; and jars break if frozen. Always label jars with the contents and the date.

DEALING WITH SPOILED FOOD

Do not take a chance on possibly spoiled low-acid canned food. Characteristics include changed color and texture, mold, bubbles in canning liquid when opening the lid, or liquid squirting out of the jar when opening. Place the jar, with the food and lid, on its side in a large stockpot or hot-water canner. Wash your hands thoroughly. Add boiling water to the pot to cover the jar by at least 1 inch (2.5 cm). Put a lid on the pot and boil rapidly for 30 minutes. You may notice an unpleasant odor. Cool and dispose of the food. Wash the containers in hot sudsy water and rinse well. Thoroughly scrub all counters, containers, and equipment that may have been in contact with the spoiled food or its container, then wash all cloths that have been used in the clean-up.

This method of canning is suitable only for high-acid foods such as fruits, pickled vegetables, and tomatoes.

Equipment

*hot-water canner
canning jars
ladle
canner rack*

HOT-WATER CANNING TIPS

❧ *A heavy stockpot of the proper size with a lid and bottom rack or a towel or cloth to keep the jars from touching the metal bottom of the pot can be used for a hot-water bath.*

❧ *Your pressure canner also can be used, without using the pressure gauge, as a regular pot for hot-water canning.*

1 **BRING WATER TO A BOIL** Start water to boil in a half-filled canner. Make sure that the water covers the jar tops by two inches (5 cm) when the canner is loaded.

2 **CHECK JARS** Check all jars for cracks or nicks. Use only new lids, discarding any that are bent or rusted. Keep clean jars and lids submerged in hot water or in the oven at 180°F (80°C) until they are ready to fill.

3 **ADD FOOD** Pack food into hot jars tightly, but not so tight that it gets crushed.

4 **CHECK HEADSPACE** Add more of the canning liquid if necessary, making certain that all jars have the correct amount of headspace (see page 65). Generally speaking, 1/2 inch (1 cm) of headspace is required but follow individual recipes carefully. Rid jars of air bubbles by jiggling a non-metal spatula along the inside of the jar. Clean the jar rims, place the lids on, and secure with screw bands. Tighten screw bands firmly, but don't use a tool or too much strength. Follow the manufacturer's instructions, enclosed with or printed on the box, for tightening lids correctly.

5 **PROCESS** Place the jars in a canner rack so that no two jars are touching. Lower the whole rack, or use a jar lifter to lower each one individually. Begin timing from when the water comes to the desired temperature. Boil or process for the time specified in the recipe. Increase the processing time by 2 minutes for each 1,000 feet (300 m) above sea level.

6 **REMOVE AND COOL** Remove the hot jars to dry on clean dish towels or a wooden rack. Again, be certain the jars aren't touching each other and see that the surface isn't too cold or drafty for the hot jars. Do not re-tighten lids. You may hear a slight pinging noise as a jar cools, indicating that a vacuum has formed, sealing the food.

7 **REMOVE SCREW RING** After 24 hours, gently remove the screw ring from each jar. Don't force them as you may break the vacuum seal.

PRESSURE CANNING

A pressure canner is always used to preserve foods with a pH value above 4.6. These foods are classified as low acid and include most vegetables, meat, and fish.

Equipment

canning jars
pressure canner
canning rack
ladle
jar lifter

QUESTIONS ABOUT HOME-CANNING SAFETY

1 Can acid be added to lower the pH of foods?

Yes. This is called acidification or pickling.

2 What about altitude's effect on hot-water canning in general?

The higher above sea level, the lower the temperature at which water boils, so the longer the food needs to be at a specific temperature to insure that bacteria are destroyed. Check with your county agent about time increases for your area.

1 **CHECK JARS** Check all jars for cracks or nicks. Use only new lids, discarding any that are bent or rusted. Keep the clean jars and lids you intend to use submerged in hot water.

2 **ADD WATER** Put 2–3 inches (5–8 cm) of water in your pressure canner and add the bottom rack.

3 **PACK VEGETABLES IN JARS** Pack cleaned and pared vegetables of like size tightly, but not crushed, into clean, hot jars. It may be desirable to blanch some vegetables for pressure canning.

4 **CHECK HEADSPACE** Add liquid, making certain all jars have the correct headspace required. Rid the jars of air bubbles by jiggling a non-metal spatula along the inside of the jar. Clean the jar rims, place lids on, and secure with screw bands. Tighten the screw bands firmly. Follow the manufacturer's instructions for tightening lids.

5 PLACE JARS IN CANNER
Put the filled, capped jars into the pressure canner, making certain that there is sufficient room for steam to circulate between each one.

6 PROCESS
Cover and secure the pressure-canner lid following the manufacturer's directions carefully. Steam should escape through the petcock for 5 minutes. This insures air is exhausted. Close the petcock or attach the weighted control (depending on your type of canner) and wait for the pressure gauge to reach the amount you need. When the pressure is correct, turn the heat down somewhat and start timing. Increase the pressure 1 lb for each 1,000 feet (300 m) above sea level (with a weighted control canner, increase pressure to the next mark), above 2,000 feet (600 m) elevation increase processing time 1/2 lb per 1,000 feet (300 m). Follow the individual recipes carefully and monitor the gauge to make certain the pressure is steady for the allotted time.

7 REST
With the lid still on, let the pressure gauge reach 0 again. Remove the lid, being careful of escaping steam.

HEADSPACE
It is essential to leave space between the top of the food and the rim of the storage container to enable a vacuum to form. Each recipe has a specified amount of headspace indicated because if too much or too little is allowed a seal will not form, causing the food to spoil. Generally speaking, 1/2 inch (1 cm) of headspace is needed.

8 COOL
Remove the jars with a jar lifter, spacing them on dry, clean dish towels or a wooden rack in a draft-free location. You may hear a slight pinging noise as the jars cool, indicating that a vacuum has formed, sealing the food. After 24 hours, gently remove the screw rings. Don't force them as you may break the seal.

Serve this colorful mixture with broiled (grilled) meat or baked eggplant (aubergine), or drain and cover with olive oil for an antipasto dish.

Equipment

baking sheet
sharp knife
chopping board
strainer
large stainless steel saucepan
5 x 1-quart (1-l)
canning jars
pressure canner
jar lifter
labels

Ingredients

6 green bell peppers
(capsicums)

10 red bell peppers
(capsicums)

8 yellow bell peppers
(capsicums)

5 teaspoons salt

5 cloves garlic

$^2/_3$ cup (5 fl oz/155 ml)
white vinegar

10 sprigs fresh tarragon

Finished Quantity
5 x 1-quart (1-l) jars

---

1 ROAST PEPPERS Preheat the oven to 400°F (200°C/Gas 6). Put the peppers on a baking sheet. Place in the oven, turning the peppers frequently, until they are black and the skin blistered. You may use the broiler (grill) for this process.

2 PEEL PEPPERS Remove the skin of the peppers and cut in half. Scrape out the seeds and pulp. It helps to do this under running water.

3 CHOP PEPPERS Cut the roasted peppers into strips or squares.

4 SOFTEN PEPPERS Put this colorful mixture into a strainer and submerge in a saucepan of boiling water for 2–3 minutes, long enough to soften slightly. Plunge immediately into cold water.

5 FILL JARS Fill each of the five clean, hot jars with 1 teaspoon of salt, 1 clove of garlic, 2 tablespoons of white vinegar, and 2 sprigs of tarragon. Then divide the pepper mixture equally among the five jars.

6 ADD BOILING WATER Fill each jar with boiling water, leaving ¹/₂ inch (1 cm) headspace.

7 REMOVE AIR BUBBLES AND SEAL Release the air bubbles in the jars by jiggling a non-metal spatula around the inside. Clean the rims and seal.

8 PROCESS AND STORE Place in a pressure canner and process at 5 lb pressure for 10 minutes. At high altitudes, increase the pressure as specified on page 65. Allow the pressure gauge to reach 0, then remove the jars from the canner and cool. Remove the screw bands after 24 hours. Check the seals, then label if desired.

Spicy Red Cabbage

This pickle is considered an "acid food" because of the vinegar it contains.

Equipment

crockery bowl
plastic cling wrap
strainer
tongs
large stainless steel saucepan
cheesecloth (muslin) square
5 x 1-quart (1-l)
canning jars
hot-water canner
jar lifter
labels

Ingredients

3 large heads red cabbage

salt

2 quarts (2 l) red wine vinegar

1 cup (6 oz / 185 g) firmly packed brown sugar

2 tablespoons mustard seeds

1 tablespoon whole cloves

1/4 cup (1 oz / 30 g) mace

3 tablespoons whole allspice

2 tablespoons peppercorns

3 tablespoons celery seeds

2 cinnamon sticks

Finished Quantity
5 x 1-quart (1-l) jars

1 SHRED AND SALT CABBAGE Core and shred the cabbage, then layer it in a crockery bowl, heavily salting each layer.

2 COVER AND SET ASIDE Cover the bowl with plastic cling wrap and put in a cool place for 24 hours.

3 DRAIN Transfer the cabbage to a strainer using tongs. Drain thoroughly for about 12 hours. Blot up excess moisture.

4 COMBINE VINEGAR, SUGAR, AND MUSTARD SEEDS In a saucepan, combine the vinegar, sugar, and mustard seeds.

5 COMBINE SPICES Tie the remaining ingredients together in a cheesecloth square and add to the pan. Boil the liquid for 5 minutes, then discard the spice bag.

9 PROCESS In a simmering (190–200°F/90–95°C) hot-water canner, process for 20 minutes. At high altitudes, increase time as specified on page 63.

6 FILL JARS Divide the cabbage equally among the five hot canning jars.

10 REMOVE JARS Remove the jars from the canner using a jar lifter, and cool.

7 ADD LIQUID Pour the hot liquid over the cabbage, leaving ¹/₂ inch (1 cm) headspace.

11 STORE After 24 hours, remove the screw bands. Check the seals, and label if desired.

8 SEAL Remove the air bubbles, clean the jar rims, and seal.

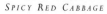

For a beautiful gift or part of a quick dinner, these carrots are enjoyed by children who hate most vegetables.

ℰ𝓆𝓊𝒾𝓅𝓂𝑒𝓃𝓉

chopping board
sharp knife
5 x 1-pint (500-ml)
canning jars
pressure canner
jar lifter
labels

ℐ𝓃𝑔𝓇𝑒𝒹𝒾𝑒𝓃𝓉𝓈

8 lb (4 kg) small carrots

5 cloves garlic

5 sprigs fresh mint, washed and cleaned

5 teaspoons fresh lemon juice

2¹/₂ teaspoons salt

1 PREPARE CARROTS Wash, peel, and chop the carrots, insuring that they are all the same size.

2 FILL JARS Pack the carrots into hot, clean jars. Add 1 clove of garlic, 1 sprig of mint, 1 teaspoon of lemon juice, and ¹/₂ teaspoon of salt to each of the five jars.

3 ADD BOILING WATER Fill each jar with boiling water, leaving ¹/₂ inch (1 cm) headspace. Release air bubbles by jiggling a non-metal spatula around the inside of the jar. Clean the jar rims and seal.

4 PROCESS AND THEN REMOVE JARS Place in a pressure canner and process at 10 lb pressure for 30 minutes. At high altitudes, increase pressure as specified on page 65. Allow the pressure gauge to return to 0, then remove the jars from the canner and cool.

5 STORE Remove the screw bands after 24 hours. Check the seals, then label if desired.

ℱ𝒾𝓃𝒾𝓈𝒽𝑒𝒹 𝒬𝓊𝒶𝓃𝓉𝒾𝓉𝓎
5 x 1-pint (500-ml) jars

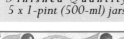
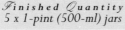
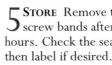

ITALIAN SAUCE

Use this versatile sauce on pizza dough, or spoon over sautéed chicken breasts and top with mozzarella cheese.

ℰquipment

large skillet (frying pan)
mixing spoon
5 x 1-pint (500-ml)
canning jars
hot-water canner
jar lifter
labels

𝒥ngredients

3 tablespoons olive oil

3 medium onions, chopped

2 cloves garlic, minced

about 30 ripe tomatoes, peeled and puréed

2 tablespoons lemon juice

1 teaspoon black pepper

2 teaspoons sugar

2 tablespoons finely chopped parsley

1 tablespoon chopped basil

1 tablespoon dried oregano

1 teaspoon celery seeds

2 teaspoons salt

𝓕inished 𝒬uantity
5 x 1-pint (500-ml) jars

1 COOK ONIONS AND GARLIC AND ADD REMAINING INGREDIENTS Heat the oil in a skillet and cook the onions and garlic until transparent. Stir in all the other ingredients. Simmer over low heat for about 2 hours or until the mixture is reduced by half, stirring often and being careful not to burn.

2 BOTTLE AND SEAL Ladle into hot, clean jars. Clean the jar rims and seal.

3 PROCESS In a gently boiling (210°F/100°C) hot-water canner, process the jars for 25 minutes. At high altitudes, increase the time as specified on page 63. Remove the jars from the canner and cool.

4 STORE After 24 hours, remove the screw bands. Check the seals, and label if desired.

BASIL TOMATO SAUCE

This sauce is a great base for baked eggplant (aubergine) topped with mozzarella.

Equipment

food processor
skillet (frying pan)
mixing spoon
ladle
2 x 1-quart (1-l) canning
jars
hot-water canner
jar lifter
labels

Ingredients

30 tomatoes

3 tablespoons olive oil

2 cloves garlic, minced

4 sprigs fresh basil, chopped

3 tablespoons finely chopped parsley

1 tablespoon lemon juice

1 teaspoon salt

2 teaspoons pepper

2 teaspoons sugar

4 teaspoons vegetable bouillon (stock) powder

Finished Quantity
2 x 1-quart (1-l) jars

1 PEEL TOMATOES Blanch the tomatoes in boiling water for 20 seconds, then plunge into cold water, drain, and peel.

2 PURÉE TOMATOES In a food processor, purée the tomatoes.

3 SAUTÉ Heat the oil in a skillet. Add the garlic, basil, and parsley and sauté, stirring occasionally.

4 ADD TOMATOES Mix in the puréed tomatoes and lemon juice.

5 ADD REMAINING INGREDIENTS Stir in the salt, pepper, sugar, and bouillon powder and simmer on low heat for 1 1/2 hours, being careful not to burn and stirring often.

6 BOTTLE Ladle into hot, clean jars leaving 1/2 inch (1 cm) headspace.

7 SEAL Release any air bubbles using a non-metal spatula. Clean the jar rims and seal.

8 PROCESS Place in a simmering (190–200°F/90–95°C) hot-water canner and process for 40 minutes. At high altitudes, increase time as specified on page 63. Remove the jars from the canner using a jar lifter, and cool.

9 STORE After 24 hours remove the screw rings. Check the seals, and label if desired.

SAFETY TIP

Dried tomatoes can be safely stored in oil without acid because they are lower in pH than the fresh tomatoes from which they were dried. If not sufficiently dried, lactic acid bacteria will cause fermentation in the jar.

VEGETABLE SOUP BASE

This is the ideal base for a delicious winter's day soup — always be sure to have a few jars on your pantry shelves.

Equipment

large stainless steel saucepan
ladle
4 x 2-quart (2-l) canning jars
pressure canner
jar lifter
labels

Ingredients

1^1/$_2$ quarts (1.5 l) water

12 large, ripe tomatoes, peeled, cored, and chopped

6 medium potatoes, peeled and cubed

1 lb (500 g) fresh lima beans

kernels from 9 ears of corn

12 medium carrots, peeled and thickly sliced

4 sticks celery, sliced

2 medium onions, chopped

2 teaspoons salt

Finished Quantity
About 4 x 2-quart (2-l) jars

1 **COMBINE INGREDIENTS EXCEPT SALT** In a large saucepan, combine all of the ingredients, except for the salt, and bring to a boil. Cook for 5 minutes.

2 **FILL JARS** Ladle the vegetable mixture into clean, hot jars, insuring that 1 inch (2.5 cm) headspace is left.

3 **ADD SALT** To each of the four jars, add ^{1}/$_2$ teaspoon salt.

SAFETY TIP
Can only as much as is needed for one season. Canned food may not be spoiled after 12 months but it might lose quality.

4 **SEAL** Release the air bubbles. Clean the jar rims and seal.

7 **STORE** Remove the screw bands after 24 hours. Check the seals, and label and date the jars.

5 **PROCESS** Place the jars in a pressure canner and process at 10 lb pressure for 1¼ hours. At high altitudes, increase pressure as specified on page 65.

6 **REMOVE JARS** Allow the pressure gauge to return to 0, then remove the jars from the canner and cool.

CANNING TIPS

❧ Always start with clean, fresh food pared to about the same size.

❧ To inactivate any botulinum toxin in spoiled food, place the jar on its side in a hot-water canner, cover with water, and boil for 30 minutes. If you notice an unpleasant odor, cool and dispose of the food.

❧ Pre-cooking the food allows a tighter pack and requires fewer jars.

❧ Always label jars with the contents and the date and store in a cool, dry, dark place.

SWEET PEPPER RELISH

A delightful gift, this piquant summer blend makes a great accompaniment for broiled (grilled) meat and poultry. My family loves it on top of black-eyed peas.

Equipment

food processor
large stainless steel saucepan
mixing spoon
7 x 1-pint (500-ml)
canning jars
hot-water canner
jar lifter
labels

Ingredients

6 lb (3 kg) red bell peppers (capsicums), seeded, and cut into small pieces

3 lb (1.5 kg) onions, peeled and cut up into medium-sized pieces

1 quart (1 l) distilled white vinegar (5% acidity)

3 cups (1½ lb/750 g) sugar

2 tablespoons salt

4 teaspoons mustard seeds

Finished Quantity
7 x 1-pint (500-ml) jars

1 PROCESS VEGETABLES Use a food processor to chop the bell peppers and onions.

2 MIX WITH REMAINING INGREDIENTS In a saucepan, combine the vegetables with the vinegar, sugar, salt, and mustard seeds.

SAFETY ADVICE

To test jar seals:
❧ *Press the middle of the lid with a finger. If it springs back when you release your finger, the lid is unsealed.*
❧ *Tap the lid with the bottom of a teaspoon. A jar that is sealed correctly will make a ringing, high-pitched sound.*
❧ *Hold the jar at eye level and look across the lid. It should be curved down slightly in the center because a vacuum has formed.*

3 **BOIL** Bring to a boil, stirring occasionally. Reduce heat to low and simmer, uncovered, being careful that the mixture doesn't stick by stirring often, for about 50–60 minutes.

4 **BOTTLE AND SEAL** Pour into hot, clean jars allowing ¹/₂ inch (1 cm) headspace. Clean the jar rims and seal.

5 **PROCESS** Place the jars in a simmering (190–200°F/90–95°C) hot-water canner and process for 15 minutes. At high altitudes, increase the time as specified on page 63.

6 **REMOVE JARS** Remove the jars from the canner and allow to cool.

7 **REMOVE SCREW RING AND STORE** After 24 hours, gently remove the screw ring from each jar. Check the seals, and label each jar. Store in a cool, dark place.

PICKLED GREEN TOMATOES

Making use of the abundance of early summer's crop, this condiment will add a lift to the turkey later in the year.

Equipment

large mixing bowl
large stainless steel saucepan
ladle
plate
weight
dish towel
serving spoon
6 x 1-quart (1-l)
canning jars
hot-water canner
labels

Ingredients

2¹/₂ lb (1.25 kg — about 100) green cherry tomatoes, washed and dried

6 sprigs fresh dill

3 tablespoons mixed pickling spice

1¹/₂ cups (12 oz / 375 g) pickling salt

2 cups (16 fl oz / 500 ml) white distilled vinegar (5% acidity)

2 quarts (2 l) water

Finished Quantity
6 x 1-quart (1-l) jars

1 COMBINE TOMATOES, DILL, AND SPICE In a bowl, layer the tomatoes, then the dill, and pickling spice.

2 COMBINE SALT, VINEGAR, AND WATER In a saucepan, make a brine of the last three ingredients, dissolving the salt and cooling slightly.

3 ADD BRINE Ladle the brine over the tomatoes.

4 **COVER** Weigh down with a plate and a heavy object. Any tomatoes left floating on top will spoil and ruin the mixture.

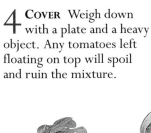

7 **BOTTLE** After 3 weeks, ladle into clean jars and seal.

5 **SET ASIDE** Cover with a dish towel and store in a cool place for about 3 weeks.

8 **PROCESS AND STORE** Place the jars in a simmering (180–190°F/ 85–90°C) hot-water canner and process for 20 minutes. At high altitudes, increase time as specified on page 63. Remove the jars from the canner and cool. Clean the rims of the jars, cover tightly, and label. This can also be stored unprocessed in the refrigerator for up to 6 months.

6 **SKIM SURFACE** Skim off scum and foam each day and place a clean plate and weight on top. Add more brine if necessary.

SPICED PEACHES

With these peaches in your pantry, delicious desserts are on hand for any occasion.

ℰquipment

large mixing bowl
large stainless steel saucepan
tongs
6 x 1-quart (1-l)
canning jars
ladle
hot-water canner
jar lifter
labels

Ingredients

24–26 large peaches, peeled

5 teaspoons (¹/₂ oz / 10 g) cloves, approximately

¹/₄ cup (2 fl oz / 60 ml) plus 2 tablespoons lemon juice

1 quart (1 l) commercial peach or apple juice

2 cups (1 lb / 500 g) sugar

1 cup (6 oz / 185 g) light brown sugar

1 stick cinnamon

Finished Quantity
6 x 1-quart (1-l) jars

1 STUD PEACHES WITH CLOVES Stick several cloves into each peach.

2 COVER PEACHES WITH WATER AND LEMON JUICE In a bowl, submerge the prepared fruit in enough water to cover. Add 2 tablespoons of the lemon juice to prevent discoloration.

3 BOIL REMAINING INGREDIENTS In a saucepan, combine the juice, sugars, remaining lemon juice, and cinnamon. Bring to a boil, stirring constantly until the sugar is dissolved.

4 ADD PEACHES
Add the peaches to the hot liquid using tongs, and heat for about 5 minutes or until the peaches are softened. Remove from heat and allow to rest overnight.

5 REMOVE CINNAMON AND REHEAT
The next day, discard the cinnamon and reheat the peaches in the syrup.

6 BOTTLE
Pack the peaches into hot, clean jars. Ladle the hot syrup over the peaches leaving ¹/4 inch (0.5 cm) headspace. Release the air bubbles in the jars.

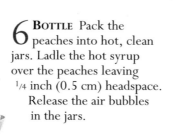

7 SEAL
Clean the jar rims and seal.

8 PROCESS
Place the jars in a gently boiling (210°F/100°C) hot-water canner and process for 25 minutes. At high altitudes, increase the time as specified on page 63. Remove the jars from the canner using a jar lifter, and cool.

9 STORE
After 24 hours remove the screw rings from each jar. Check the seals, and label if desired.

CHRISTMAS PEARS

If you can part with these pears, they are definitely a great gift idea. Arrange them on fresh curly kale in a wreath shape for a colorful buffet table presentation.

Equipment

chopping board
sharp knife
large mixing bowl
large stainless steel saucepan
ladle
6 x 1-pint (500-ml)
canning jars
hot-water canner
labels

Ingredients

12 large, perfectly ripe pears

1 tablespoon lemon juice

2¹/3 cups (7 oz/220 g) cinnamon-heart red-hot candies

1¹/4 quarts (1.25 l) water

1 tablespoon fruit color protector (such as Fresh Fruit)

2 drops red food coloring

Finished Quantity
6 x 1-pint (500-ml) jars

1 PEEL, CORE, AND HALVE PEARS Remove the skin of the pears, core them, and cut in half. Combine the lemon juice with enough water to cover the pear halves and submerge them in the liquid to avoid discoloration.

2 BOIL CANDIES AND WATER In a saucepan, boil the candies in the water, stirring until completely dissolved.

HOT-PACK BENEFITS

Hot-packed food has superior color and flavor to raw-packed food and is ideal for hot-water canning as it:
- *Helps to remove air from food tissues.*
- *Shrinks food.*
- *Increases the vacuum in sealed jars.*
- *Prevents food from floating in the jars.*

3 ADD FRUIT COLOR PROTECTOR AND FOOD COLORING

Add the fruit color protector and food coloring. Stir until completely dissolved, about 2 minutes.

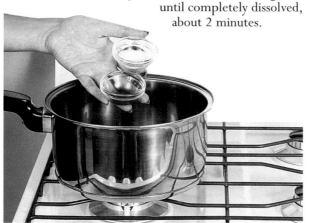

4 ADD PEARS

Drain the pear halves, add to the saucepan and cook for 3–4 minutes or until the pears are heated through.

5 BOTTLE

Ladle the fruit into the jars and top up with the red cooking liquid.

6 SEAL

Release the air bubbles from the jars. Clean the jar rims and seal.

7 PROCESS

Place the jars in a gently boiling (210°F/100°C) hot-water canner and process for 20 minutes. At high altitudes, increase the time as specified on page 63. Remove the jars from the canner using a jar lifter, and cool.

8 STORE

After 24 hours remove the screw bands. Check the seals on the jars, and label if desired.

APPLE-PIE FILLING

A tried-and-tested favorite, a supply of this filling makes pie-making a piece of cake!

ℰ q u i p m e n t

*large stainless steel saucepan
mixing spoon
tongs
1 x 1-quart (1-l) canning jar
hot-water canner
jar lifter
label*

ℐ n g r e d i e n t s

³/₄ cup (6 oz/185 g) sugar

¹/₄ cup (1¹/₂ oz/45 g) Clear Jel-A (modified cornstarch/cornflour) or quick-cooking tapioca

pinch ground cinnamon

¹/₈ teaspoon nutmeg

¹/₂ cup (4 fl oz/125 ml) cold water

³/₄ cup (6 fl oz/185 ml) apple juice

2 tablespoons lemon juice

4 cooking apples, peeled, cored, sliced, and blanched for 1 minute

ℱ i n i s h e d 𝒬 u a n t i t y
1-quart (1-l)

---

1 COMBINE SUGAR, CLEAR JEL-A, SPICES, WATER, AND APPLE JUICE In a saucepan, mix the sugar, Clear Jel-A, and spices with the water and apple juice. Stir on medium heat until the mixture begins to bubble and thicken, being careful not to burn.

2 ADD LEMON JUICE Stir in the lemon juice and boil for 1 minute.

PREPARATION TIPS

❧ *Our Golden Delicious apples are ready for enjoying in fall, so be sure to use your surplus to make apple-pie fillings.*
❧ *If processing a full canner load of jars, keep blanched apples warm in a covered pot.*
❧ *Keep raw apples covered with 4 quarts (4 l) of water and ¹/₂ teaspoon of ascorbic acid to prevent browning.*

3 ADD APPLES
Immediately add the still-warm apple slices.

6 PROCESS, THEN REMOVE JARS
Place in a gently boiling (210°F/100°C) hot-water canner and process for 25 minutes. At high altitudes, increase time as specified on page 63. Remove the jars from the canner with a jar lifter, and cool.

4 BOTTLE
Fill a clean, hot jar with the apple mixture using tongs, leaving a 2-inch (5-cm) headspace.

7 STORE
After 24 hours remove the screw rings. Check the jar seals, and label if desired.

5 SEAL
Clean the rim of the jar and seal.

APPLE-PIE FILLING

LEMON CURD

An old-fashioned favorite, lemon curd never goes out of style. All you need is a sweet pastry shell to complete an easy, rich dessert.

Equipment

double boiler
mixing spoon
ladle
4 x 1-pint (500-ml)
canning jars
hot-water canner
jar lifter
labels

Ingredients

4 large lemons

2½ cups (10 oz/315 g) sugar cubes

¾ cup (6 oz/185 g) sweet (unsalted) butter

7 eggs, beaten and strained

PREPARATION TIP

Try combining fresh orange or lime juice with the lemon juice for a different taste sensation.

Finished Quantity
4 x 1-pint (500-ml) jars

1 **RUB LEMONS WITH SUGAR, THEN COMBINE ALL INGREDIENTS** Rub the whole lemons with the sugar cubes until the sugar is soaked with lemon oil. Juice the lemons and strain. In the top of a double boiler, combine the lemon-oil soaked sugar cubes, lemon juice, butter, and eggs. Stir constantly until thick. Do not over-cook.

2 **BOTTLE AND SEAL** Ladle the hot lemon curd into clean, hot jars. Clean the jar rims and seal.

3 **PROCESS** Place the jars in a simmering (190–200°F/90–95°C) hot-water canner and process for 20 minutes. At high altitudes, increase the time as specified on page 63. Remove the jars from the canner and cool.

4 **STORE** After 24 hours remove the screw rings. Check the seals on the jars, and label if desired.

ORANGE SYRUP

Use this over buttermilk pancakes and sprinkle fresh blueberries on top for a special Sunday brunch.

Equipment

large stainless steel saucepan
ladle
strainer
cheesecloth (muslin)
mixing bowl
4 x 1-pint (500-ml) canning jars
hot-water canner
jar lifter
labels

Ingredients

zest (rind) of 6 oranges such as Valencia, cut in strips

1 quart (1 l) water

4 cups (2 lb/1 kg) sugar

2 cups (16 fl oz/500 ml) fresh orange juice from oranges above, strained

2 tablespoons citric acid

Finished Quantity
4 x 1-pint (500-ml) jars

1 BOIL ZEST, WATER, AND SUGAR In a saucepan, boil the zest, water, and sugar, stirring constantly until the sugar is dissolved, then boil without stirring for 3 minutes.

2 COOL Remove from the heat, cool, cover, and stand for 12 hours.

3 STRAIN Ladle the zest mixture into a strainer lined with several layers of cheesecloth, and press the liquid into a bowl.

4 ADD ORANGE JUICE AND CITRIC ACID

Mix in the orange juice and citric acid.

5 REHEAT Pour the syrup back into the saucepan and reheat.

6 BOTTLE Ladle the syrup into hot, clean jars leaving ½ inch (1 cm) headspace.

7 SEAL Clean the jar rims and seal. Loosen the screw bands by half a turn.

8 PROCESS Place the jars in a gently boiling (210°F/100°C) hot-water canner and process for 30 minutes. At high altitudes, increase time as specified on page 63.

9 REMOVE JARS Remove the jars from the canner and re-tighten the lids.

10 STORE After 24 hours, remove the screw bands. Check the seals and label the jars, if desired. The unprocessed syrup will keep for up to 21 days in the refrigerator.

ITALIAN STRAWBERRY SYRUP

This recipe can be transformed into a refreshing wine, sparkling-water drink, or a delightful granita.

Equipment

food processor
large mixing bowl
mixing spoon
dish towel
cheesecloth (muslin)
large stainless steel saucepan
2 x 1-quart (1-l) canning jars
hot-water canner
label

Ingredients

2 lb (1 kg) ripe strawberries, hulled and washed

2 packages active dry yeast

6 cups (3 lb / 1.5 kg) plus 1 teaspoon sugar

1 quart (1 l) water

1¹/₂ cups (12 fl oz / 375 ml) lemon juice (bottled may be used)

Finished Quantity
2 x 1-quart (1-l) jars

1 PURÉE Process the strawberries in a food processor until puréed.

2 COMBINE STRAWBERRIES, YEAST, AND SUGAR In a bowl, mix the strawberries, yeast, and the 1 teaspoon of sugar. Stir until the yeast is dissolved.

3 COVER Cover with a clean dish towel and set aside at room temperature to ferment. Stir occasionally.

4 STRAIN Once the mixture no longer bubbles when stirred (after about 4 days), strain through layers of cheesecloth into a large saucepan. Squeeze the cheesecloth to extract all the juice.

5 ADD REMAINING INGREDIENTS, AND REDUCE To the strawberry mixture in the saucepan add the remaining ingredients. Bring to a boil and reduce to about 7 cups (1¾ quarts/1.75 l) of liquid.

6 COOL AND POUR INTO JARS Remove from the heat and allow to cool. Then, if you intend to use all the syrup within 1 month, simply pour the cooled mixture into clean glass containers. Without further processing, the syrup will keep, refrigerated, for up to 4 weeks.

SHOPPING ADVICE

❧ Select fruit that is just ripe (under- rather than overripe) and in perfect condition, that is, free from bruises.

❧ Watch out for the tiny juicier berries of the early season — they make a sweeter syrup.

7 PROCESS AND STORE To keep the syrup longer than 1 month, place the jars in a gently boiling (210°F/100°C) hot-water canner and process for 15 minutes. At high altitudes, increase time as specified on page 63. Remove the jars from the canner, cover tightly. After 24 hours remove the screw rings. Check the seals and label, if desired. Do not shake the syrup but allow the sediment to remain on the bottom.

Processing Time for Hot-water Canning *(in minutes)*				
Fruits	*Type of Pack*	*¹/₂ pint* (1 cup/250 ml)	*1 pint* (2 cups/500 ml)	*1 quart* (4 cups/1 l)
Apples	Hot	15	20	20
Apricots	Raw	20	25	30
	Hot	15	20	25
Berries	Raw	10	15	20
	Hot	10	10	15
Cherries	Raw	20	25	25
	Hot	10	15	20
Currants	Raw	10	15	20
Dried fruits	Raw	10	15	20
Grapefruit	Raw	10	10	10
Grapes	Raw	10	15	20
Guavas	Hot	10	15	20
Loquats	Hot	10	15	20
Mixed fruits	Hot	15	20	25
Nectarines	Raw	20	25	30
Peaches	Raw	20	25	30
	Hot	15	20	25
Pears	Hot	15	20	25
Pineapple	Hot	10	15	20
Plums	Hot	15	20	25
Tomatoes	Hot	40	40	45

Vegetables (low acid)	Type of Pack	¹/₂ pint (1 cup/250 ml)	1 pint (2 cups/500 ml)	1 quart (4 cups/1 l)
		Processing time at 10 lb (240°F/115°C at sea level)		
Asparagus	Raw or hot	30	30	40
Beans, green or yellow	Raw or hot	20	20	25
Beans, lima and butter	Raw or hot	40	40	50
Beets (beetroot)	Hot	30	30	35
Carrots	Raw or hot	25	25	30
Corn	Raw or hot	55	55	85
Okra	Hot	25	25	40
Peas, blackeye, crowder, field	Raw or hot	35	35	40
Peas, green	Raw or hot	40	40	40
Peppers, bell* (capsicums)	Hot	35	35	10
Potatoes	Hot	35	35	40
Potatoes, sweet	Hot and wet	55	55	90
Rutabaga (swede)	Hot	30	30	35
Salsify	Hot	25	25	35
Spinach	Hot	70	70	90
Squash, summer (pattypan squash)	Hot	30	30	40
Turnips	Hot	30	30	35

*process at 5 lb pressure

Mail Order Sources

Altrusa Corporation
Ball Home Canning
Products,
Consumer Affairs Dept.
P. O. Box 2729
Muncie, IN 47307
(317) 281-5009

Compliments to the Chef
374 Merriman Ave
Ashville, NC 28801
(704) 258-0558
(800) 895-CHEF

Macy's
The Marketplace
151 West 34th Street
New York, NY 10001
(212) 695-4400
(800) 456-2297

Williams-Sonoma
Mail Order Department
P. O. Box 7456
San Francisco, CA
94120-7456
(415) 652-9007
(800) 541-2233

Mail Order Seeds and Plants

The Herbfarm
32804 Issaquah/Fall City
Road, Fall City,
WA 98024

Le Jardin du Gourmet
West Danville, VT 05873

Sandy Mush Herb
Nursery
316 Surrett Cove Road
Leicester, NC 28748
(704) 683-2014

Shady Hill Gardens
803 Walnut Street
Batavia, IL 60510
(312) 879-5665

Shepherd's Garden Seeds
Shipping Office
30 Irene Street
Torrington, CT 06790
(203) 482-3638

A Bibliography of Additional Reading

Andrews, Glenn. *Making and Using Flavored Vinegars.* Pownal, VT: Garden Way Publishing, 1991, Pub. #A112

Creber, Ann. *Oils and Vinegars.* Rutland, VT: Charles E. Tuttle Co., 1992

Freid, Mimi. *Making Liqueurs for Gifts.* Pownal, VT: Garden Way Publishing, 1991, Pub. #A101

Gunst, Kathy. *Condiments.* New York: G. P. Putnam's Sons, 1984

Hopley, Claire. *Making and Using Mustards.* Pownal, VT: Garden Way Publishing, 1991, Pub. #A129

Oster, Maggie. *Herbal Vinegar.* Pownal, VT: Storey Publishing, 1994

Tolley, Emelie & Chris Mead. *The Herbal Pantry.* New York: Clarkson N. Potter, Inc., 1992

Van Garde, Shirley. *Food Preservation and Safety: Principles and Practice,* Iowa State University Press, 1994

INDEX

acidity 58
apples
  apple-crumb pie 32–33
  apple-pie filling 84–85
  dried apple rings 48
  drying 52
  freezing 34
  hot-water canning 92
apricots
  drying 52
  freezing 34
  hot-water canning 92
  oven-dried 43
artichokes, freezing 34
asparagus
  drying 52
  freezing 34
  pressure canning 93
aspartame 12
aubergine, *see* eggplant
avocados
  freezing 34
  purée 27

bacteria 57, 58
bananas
  drying 52
  freezing 34
basil tomato sauce 72–73
beans
  drying 52
  freezing 34
  pressure canning 93
  see also butter beans; green
    beans; lima beans; string
    beans
beetroot, *see* beets
beets
  drying 52
  pressure canning 93
bell peppers
  drying 54
  freezing 37
  pressure canning 93
  roasted 66–67
  sweet relish 76–77
berries
  freezing 34
  hot-water canning 92
blackberries, drying not
  recommended 55
blanching 17–18, 39–40
blueberries, drying 52
bottling, as a term 13
  see also canning
botulism 57, 58
broccoli
  drying 52
  freezing 34
Brussels sprouts
  drying not recommended 55

freezing 34
butter beans, pressure canning
  93

cabbage
  drying 52
  freezing 34
  spicy red 68–69
canning 57–93
  canning and bottling 13
  equipment 59–60
  hot-climate fruits 58
  hot-water canning 57, 62–63
  pressure canning 57, 64–65
  procedures 60–61
  processing time chart 92–93
  recipes 66–91
  spoiled food 61
  storage 61
capsicums, *see* bell peppers
carrots
  drying 52
  freezing 34
  minted 70
  pressure canning 93
casserole, Vidalia onion 24–25
cauliflower
  drying 52
  freezing 35
celeriac, freezing 35
celery
  drying 52
  freezing 35
cherries
  drying 52
  freezing 35
  hot-water canning 92
chilies
  drying 54
  freezing 37
citrus fruit, freezing 35
citrus peel, drying 52
Clostridium botulinum 57, 58
coconut
  drying 53
  freezing 35
corn
  drying 53
  freezing 35
  pressure canning 93
courgettes, *see* zucchini
cranberries, freezing 35
cucumber, drying 53
currants, hot-water canning 92

dates, drying 53
dried fruits, hot-water canning
  92
dry pack, for fruit 18
drying 39–55
  chart of specific fruits and
    vegetables 52–55
  methods 40–41

pasteurization and storing
  41–42
  preparations 39–40
  recipes 43–51
  rehydrating 42
  sulfuring 40

eggplant
  caviar 22–23
  drying 53
  freezing 35
equipment
  canning 59–60
  freezing 15–16

figs
  drying 53
  freezing 35
freezing 15–37
  chart of specific fruits and
    vegetables 34–37
  cooking frozen vegetables 17
  equipment 15–16
  packaging 16–17
  preparing fruits 18–19
  preparing vegetables 17–18
  recipes 20–33
  safety precautions 17

garlic
  drying 53
  freezing 35
gazpacho 26
glucose 11
grape leaves, freezing 36
grapefruit, hot-water
  canning 92
grapes
  drying 53
  freezing 36
  hot-water canning 92
green beans
  drying 52
  pressure canning 93
guavas, hot-water canning 92

headspace
  canning 65
  freezing 16
herbs
  dried, in bags 45
  freezing 20, 36
  oven-dried 49
  sun-dried 43
honey 11–12
horseradish, drying 53
hot pack, canning 60–61
hot-climate fruits, canning 58
hot-water canning 57, 62–63

Italian sauce 71
Italian strawberry syrup 90–91

jar seals 60

kiwi fruit, freezing 36
kohlrabi, freezing 36
labeling, canned fruits and
  vegetables 61
leather britches 44
leeks
  drying 53
  freezing 36
lemon curd 86
lettuce, drying not
  recommended 55
lids 60
light corn syrup 11
lima beans
  drying 52
  pressure canning 93
loquats, hot-water canning 92
low-acid foods 13, 59

melons, freezing 36
microwave blanching 18
mixed fruits, hot-water
  canning 92
mushrooms
  air-dried 51
  drying 53
  freezing 36

nectarines
  drying 53
  freezing 36
  hot-water canning 92

oils 12
okra
  drying 53
  freezing 36
  pressure canning 93
onions
  drying 53
  freezing 36
  Vidalia onion casserole 24–25
orange syrup 88–89
oven-drying 41

packaging, for freezing 16–17
papaya, drying 53
parsnips
  drying 54
  freezing 37
pasteurizing 41–42
pattypan squash, see summer
  squash
pawpaw, see papaya
peaches
  drying 53
  freezing 36
  hot-water canning 92
  spiced 80–81
pears
  Christmas 82–83
  drying 54
  freezing 37

hot-water canning 92
peas
  drying 44, 54
  freezing 37
  pressure canning 93
peppers, see bell peppers,
  chilies
pickled green tomatoes 78–79
pineapple
  drying 54
  freezing 37
  hot-water canning 92
plums
  drying 54
  freezing 37
  hot-water canning 92
potatoes
  drying 54
  oven-baked 30–31
  pressure canning 93
  see also sweet potatoes
preserving
  preparations 10–11
  see also canning; drying;
    freezing
pressure canning 57, 64–65
pumpkin
  drying 54
  freezing 37
  soup 28

radish, drying not
  recommended 55
raspberries, drying not
  recommended 55
raw pack, canning 61
reconstituting 42
rehydrating 42
rhubarb
  drying 54
  freezing 37
rutabaga
  freezing 36
  pressure canning 93

safety precautions
  canning 59
  freezing 17
salsify, pressure canning 93
salt 11
silverbeet, drying 54
soups
  gazpacho 26
  summer squash 28
  vegetable base 74–75
spices 12
spinach
  drying 54
  freezing 37
  pressure canning 93
squash

drying 55
  pressure canning 93
  soup 28
steam blanching 18, 39–40
storage
  canned fruits and vegetables 61
  dried fruits and vegetables
    41–42
  frozen fruits and vegetables
    16–17
strawberries
  drying 54
  Italian syrup 90–91
string beans, drying 44
sugar 11
sugar syrup, wet packs 18
sulfuring 40
summer squash
  drying 55
  pressure canning 93
  soup 28
sun-drying 40–41
swede, see rutabaga
sweet potatoes
  drying 54
  pressure canning 93
  pudding 21
sweet salad onions 24–25
sweeteners 11–12
Swiss chard, drying 54

temperature
  for canning 57, 58
  for drying 40, 41
  for freezing 15
tomatoes
  basil tomato sauce 72–73
  canning 58
  drying 54
  freezing 37
  gazpacho 26
  hot-water canning 92
  Italian sauce 71
  marinated sun-dried 46–47
  oven-dried 50
  pickled green 78–79
tropical fruits, canning 58
turnips
  drying 55
  freezing 37
  pressure canning 93

vacuum sealing 17
vegetable soup base 74–75
Vidalia onion casserole 24–25
vinegars 12–13

water, purity of 12
wet pack, for fruit 18–19

zucchini
  drying 55
  freezing 37